A Reader's Guide to
CALVIN'S
Institutes

Published by Baker Academic
a division of Baker Publishing Group
P.O. Box 6287, Grand Rapids, MI 49516-6287
www.bakeracademic.com

Printed in the United States of America

Library of Congress Cataloging-in-Publication Data
Lane, A. N. S.
    A reader's guide to Calvin's Institutes / Anthony N. S. Lane.
        p.   cm.
    Includes bibliographical references.
    ISBN 978-0-8010-3731-3 (pbk.)
    1. Calvin, Jean, 1509–1564. Institutio Christianae religionis. 2. Reformed Church—Doctrines. 3. Theology, Doctrinal. I. Title.
    BX9420.I69L36 2009
    230'.42—dc22   2009005549

Contents

List of Abbreviations   7
How to Use This Book   9
John Calvin and His *Institutes*   11
Introduction to the Notes   23

Reading Guide
1. Introductory Material (pp. 3–8; "Prefatory Address")   27

Book 1: The Knowledge of God the Creator   33
2. Knowing God and Ourselves (1.1–4)   35
3. God Revealed in Creation (1.5)   38
4. The Bible and the Holy Spirit (1.6–9)   42
5. Idolatry and the Trinity (1.11–13)   49
6. The Created World and Humanity as Created (1.14–15)   53
7. God's Sovereign Providence (1.16–18)   57

Book 2: The Knowledge of God the Redeemer in Christ   63
8. Original Sin (2.1–2.3.5)   65
9. How God Works in the Human Heart (2.3.6–2.5)   71
10. The Place of the Law (2.6–7)   75

5

11. Exposition of the Moral Law (2.8)   79
12. Relation between the Old and New Testaments (2.9–11)   83
13. The Person of Jesus Christ (2.12–14)   87
14. The Redemptive Work of Jesus Christ (2.15–17)   91

Book 3: The Way in Which We Receive the Grace of Christ   95

15. Saving Faith (3.1–2)   97
16. Regeneration and Repentance (3.3–5)   101
17. The Christian Life: Self-Denial (3.6–7)   105
18. The Christian Life: Bearing Our Cross and Attitude toward This Life (3.8–10)   108
19. Justification by Faith (3.11.1–3.14.8)   112
20. The Value of Our Good Works (3.14.9–3.18)   116
21. The True Nature of Christian Freedom (3.19)   121
22. Prayer (3.20)   124
23. Election and Reprobation (3.21–23)   128
24. Predestination and the Final Resurrection (3.24–25)   132

Book 4: The External Means or Aids   137

25. The True Church (4.1)   139
26. The Roman Church and the Christian Ministry (4.2–7)   143
27. The Authority of the Church (4.8–9)   148
28. Church Discipline (4.10–13)   151
29. The Sacraments in General (4.14; 4.19)   155
30. Baptism and Infant Baptism (4.15–16)   159
31. The Lord's Supper (4.17–18)   163
32. Civil Government (4.20)   170

Appendix: Table of Reading Lengths   173

Abbreviations

§/§§	section/sections
bk./bks.	book/books
MB	McNeill-Battles translation of the 1559 edition of Calvin's *Institutes* (published by Westminster, 1960)
n./nn.	note/notes
p./pp.	page/pages
par./pars.	paragraph/paragraphs
sent./sents.	sentence/sentences

How to Use This Book

Calvin's *Institutes* is one of the great classics of Christian theology. This volume is designed as a guide to reading it in the McNeill-Battles translation (hereafter, MB). It is not a book to be read in its own right but functions purely as a reading guide. There are many other books about Calvin in general and about the *Institutes* in particular, but none of these actually guides the reader through a reading of the text, with direction as to the key sections to read. The notes are almost entirely devoted to expounding the *Institutes*, but I do occasionally discuss how the teaching might apply to today and also occasionally offer critical comments.

This volume guides the reader specifically through MB in that there are numerous references to the wording of this translation, to specific pages and paragraphs, and to the footnotes. Where there is, below, a simple reference to "p. *x*" or "n. *y*," this refers to the relevant page or footnote in this translation. This volume could be used in conjunction with a different translation of the *Institutes*, but a significant amount of material would then no longer be relevant.

The *Institutes* is divided into thirty-two portions, in addition to Calvin's introductory material. From each of these an average of some eighteen pages has been selected to be read. These selections are designed to cover the whole range of the *Institutes*, to cover all of Calvin's positive theology, while missing most of his polemics against his opponents and most of the historical material. My notes concentrate on the sections chosen for reading but also contain brief summaries of the other material.

Readers have four options:

1. Read only the selected material and my brief summaries of the rest.
2. Read only the selected material and use Battles's *Analysis of the Institutes*[1] as a summary of the rest.
3. Concentrate on the selected material but skim through the rest.
4. Read the whole of the *Institutes*.

The notes guide the reader through the text and also draw attention to the most significant footnotes in the Battles edition. At the beginning of each portion is an introduction and a question or questions to focus the mind of the reader.

For those who wish to read further, many books expound the whole of Calvin's theology, but I shall mention only three.

F. Wendel's *Calvin* (London: Collins, 1963) was originally written in French in 1950. Even after more than half a century, this remains arguably the best general introduction to Calvin, with a brief account of his life and of the development of the *Institutes*, together with a superb account of his theology.

T. H. L. Parker's *Calvin: An Introduction to His Thought*, Outstanding Christian Thinkers Series (London: Geoffrey Chapman, 1995), is especially relevant for our present purposes since it sets out to expound the theology of the *Institutes* in particular, rather than Calvin's thought in general.

C. Partee's *The Theology of John Calvin* (Louisville: Westminster John Knox, 2008) is a substantial exposition of Calvin's theology. It is the latest addition to the genre and a worthy one.

---

1. F. L. Battles, *Analysis of the Institutes of the Christian Religion of John Calvin* (Grand Rapids: Baker, 1980; Phillipsburg, NJ: P&R, 2001).

John Calvin and His *Institutes*

John Calvin was born in 1509 at Noyon, in northern France.[1] He studied at Paris, Orleans, and Bourges universities and became an admirer of Erasmus and humanism. In 1532 he produced a work of humanist scholarship, a commentary on the Roman philosopher Seneca's *Clemency*, which failed to make the impact for which he had hoped. At about this time, Calvin was converted to the Protestant cause. In his own words:

> Since I was too obstinately devoted to the superstitions of Popery to be easily extricated from so profound an abyss of mire, God by a sudden conversion subdued and brought my mind to a teachable frame, which was more hardened in such matters than might have been expected from one at my early period of life.[2]

He immediately devoted himself to theological study. In 1533, he was associated with a mildly Protestant speech given by the new rector of the University of Paris, Nicholas Cop. Calvin had to leave town in a hurry. The following year a number

1. The first section, on Calvin's life and works, is drawn heavily from my *A Concise History of Christian Thought* (London: T&T Clark [Continuum], 2006), 174–78, for which the publishers have kindly granted permission.
2. J. Calvin, *Commentary on the Book of Psalms*, trans. J. Anderson (Grand Rapids: Eerdmans, 1949), 1:xl ("Author's Preface").

of "Placards" attacking the Roman Mass were posted around Paris—one on the door of the royal bedchamber, if the report is to be believed. The king, Francis I, was furious and launched a vigorous onslaught on the Evangelicals. Calvin left France and settled in Basel to study and to write. By the summer of 1535, he had finished the first edition of his *Institutes*. But this peaceful period of scholarship was to be short. In 1536, he was on his way to Strassburg[3] when a local war forced him to make a detour through Geneva—the most fateful traffic diversion in European history, as has been said. Geneva had just accepted the Reformation, partly for political reasons. Calvin planned to spend only one night there, but William Farel, the leader of the Genevan Reformers, came to urge him to stay. As Calvin put it:

> After having learned that my heart was set upon devoting myself to private studies, for which I wished to keep myself free from other pursuits, and finding that he gained nothing by entreaties, [Farel] proceeded to utter an imprecation that God would curse my retirement, and the tranquillity of the studies which I sought, if I should withdraw and refuse to give assistance, when the necessity was so urgent. By this imprecation I was so stricken with terror, that I desisted from the journey which I had undertaken.[4]

The city council noticed the employment of "that Frenchman." Calvin ministered in Geneva from 1536 to 1538. But at this stage, he was still impetuous and immature. Conflict over the issue of church government led to his exile, and he withdrew to Basel to resume his studies. But again this was not to be. Martin Bucer urged him to come to Strassburg to minister to the small congregation of French refugees. Calvin resisted until Bucer took a leaf out of Farel's book and threatened him with the example of Jonah. Calvin reluctantly gave way. Apart from poverty, his

---

3. Throughout this reader, I have used the German spelling for the city of Strasbourg as a reminder that it was a German city in Calvin's day.
4. Ibid., xlii–xliii.

years at Strassburg were not unpleasant. He enjoyed his contact with Bucer and the other Reformers and profited greatly from it. He was able to take part in the colloquies between Protestants and Roman Catholics in the years 1539 to 1541, becoming well acquainted with Philipp Melanchthon in the process. He also acquired a wife, the widow of a convert from Anabaptism. But while Calvin was at Strassburg, the church at Geneva was going from bad to worse. Eventually, in 1540, the magistrates in desperation asked Calvin to return. He was appalled, having earlier stated about the prospect of a return to Geneva, "I would prefer a hundred other deaths to that cross, on which I should have to die a thousand times a day."[5] Yet after consideration, "a solemn and conscientious regard to my duty prevailed with me to consent to return to the flock from which I had been torn— but with what grief, tears, great anxiety and distress I did this, the Lord is my best witness."[6]

Calvin returned to Geneva in 1541. His fears were amply justified. There was to be a long and bitter struggle in which Calvin fought for the spiritual independence of the Genevan church and for the imposition of a rigorous discipline. The rules that he sought to impose (including regulation of dress and prohibition of dancing) were mostly traditional medieval laws. The novelty lay in his determination actually to enforce them and to do so on the *whole* of Genevan society, not exempting the ruling classes. For many years, Calvin had to face intense opposition from the magistrates, but eventually his opponents were discredited, and there was a pro-Calvin city council. In the final years of his life, he was highly respected, though his wishes were not always obeyed. He died in 1564.

Calvin has not had a good press. In 1559 he claimed that "there is no one who is assailed, bitten, and wounded by more false accusations than I" (MB, p. 4). These words were to be more prophetic than he could have realized. He is blamed for the doctrine of predestination, so clearly taught by Augustine,

5. Cited in F. Wendel, *Calvin* (London: Collins, 1963), 67.
6. Calvin, *Commentary on Psalms*, xliv ("Author's Preface").

by most medieval theologians, and by all the Reformers. It is true that Calvin heightened it somewhat, but no more than had some medieval theologians, such as Bradwardine. He is vilified for his part in the execution of the heretic Servetus (for denying the doctrine of the Trinity)—although his contemporaries applauded him almost to a man and although many of those considered saintly today (such as Thomas More) persecuted heretics more fiercely than did Calvin. Calvin must be judged against the background of his times. He is accused of being the "dictator of Geneva"—while even at the height of his power, his authority was primarily moral rather than legal, and he even had to seek the approval of the city council before publishing his books. Of course he was not perfect. Calvin acknowledged that he suffered from a bad temper. He was intolerant, assuming too readily that opposition to *his* teaching was opposition to *God's* Word—a fault shared by many others then and now. To some extent Calvin's ill repute is the fault of his disciples, who often upset the careful balance of his theology by making the doctrine of predestination central and foundational whereas Calvin was careful to keep it in its place.

Calvin transformed Geneva. The Scots Reformer John Knox declared it to be "the most perfect school of Christ that ever was in earth since the days of the Apostles. In other places, I confess Christ to be truly preached; but manners and religion so sincerely reformed, I have not yet seen in any other place."[7] This was the result of Calvin's rigorous discipline. For those who disliked it, Calvin suggested that if they did not want to live under the yoke of Christ, they should build another city where they could live as they wished. It was also the result of a massive influx of French and other refugees into the tiny city, drawn mostly by their admiration of Calvin. Calvin's primary concern was for his homeland (France), and many who came to Geneva returned to pastor the growing number of French Protestant churches. Calvin founded an academy to train them,

7. J. Ridley, *John Knox* (Oxford: Oxford University Press, 1968), 215.

the precursor of the modern university of Geneva, drawing upon the educational pattern that he had seen in Strassburg.

Calvin claimed, with some justice, that "by nature I love brevity" (MB, p. 685). Yet he was one of the most prolific writers in the history of the church. His output would have been remarkable for a full-time scholar, yet Calvin fitted it into a schedule that would have exhausted two lesser men. Apart from his many responsibilities at Geneva, he was the most important leader of the international network of Reformed churches. His letters fill many large volumes, and a list of their recipients would read like a *Who's Who* of Reformation Europe.

Calvin wrote many polemical treatises. Several of these were directed against Anabaptism. More important were his attacks on Roman Catholicism. In 1539, after Calvin had been exiled from Geneva, Cardinal Sadolet wrote to the Genevans, urging them to return to the Roman fold. The letter was forwarded to Calvin, who (in a mere six days) wrote a *Reply to Sadolet*, one of his best works. He also published the *Acts* of the early sessions of the Council of Trent—with an *Antidote*. Calvin was capable of satire as biting as any from Erasmus, as can be seen from his *Admonition in Which It Is Shown How Advantageous for Christendom Would Be an Inventory of the Bodies and Relics of Saints*, known as the *Treatise on Relics*.

Against his will, Calvin also found himself forced to write against Lutherans. After he reached his 1549 *Zurich Agreement* with Bullinger on the doctrine of the Lord's Supper, two Lutheran pastors, Westphal and Hesshusius, attacked him, and Calvin responded. The controversy grieved him because he saw himself as a disciple of Luther. Not all of Calvin's treatises were polemical. One of the finest is a *Short Treatise on the Lord's Supper*, which sets out his teaching in a conciliatory fashion, as the middle way between Zwingli and Luther. Luther himself is reported to have spoken appreciatively of it.

Calvin preached regularly throughout his time at Geneva. From 1549, his sermons were recorded in shorthand. A number were published in the sixteenth century, but the majority remained in the Genevan library in shorthand form. Incredibly,

15

these were sold off by weight in 1805, and three-quarters of them are lost. Those that survive are now being published.

Calvin wrote commentaries on many of the books of the Bible: Genesis to Joshua, Psalms, all of the prophets except Ezekiel 21–48, and all of the New Testament except 2 and 3 John and Revelation. These commentaries were often based on earlier sermons or lectures. Calvin's commentaries are among the very few written before the nineteenth century that are still of value for understanding the meaning of the text (as opposed to those that might be read today for edification rather than for the light that they shed on the text of the Bible). He is the only writer ever to belong without question both to the first rank of theologians *and* to the first rank of commentators.

Calvin is best known for his *Instruction in the Christian Religion* (commonly called the *Institutes*). Written in Latin, it went through five major editions, listed below. He was revising it for most of his literary and pastoral life. Like Augustine, he was one of those who write as they learn and learn as they write (MB, p. 5).[8]

Editions of the *Institutes*

1536 Edition

This was probably completed by August 23, 1535, the date of the "Prefatory Address." It was published the following March in Basel, in a pocketbook format. It was roughly as long as the section of the New Testament from Matthew to Ephesians. There were six chapters. Four cover the law, the Apostles' Creed, the Lord's Prayer, and the sacraments (baptism and Lord's Supper)—the traditional components of a catechism. The other two chapters—on the false (Roman Catholic) sacraments and on Christian liberty—were more polemical in tone, as was the "Prefatory Address to King Francis I."

8. For more on the editions of the *Institutes*, see pp. xxix–xxxviii; Wendel, *Calvin*, 111–22, 144–49; R. A. Muller, *The Unaccommodated Calvin* (New York: Oxford University Press, 2000), chaps. 6–7. For the meaning of the word *Institutio*, see p. xxxi, n. 3.

1539 Edition

This was nearly completed by October 1, 1538, and was published the following August in Strassburg. It was nearly three times as long as the first edition, the six chapters having become seventeen. It was a thorough revision of the first edition, and the title page states that it "now, at last corresponds to its title." There was a French translation, which appeared in 1541, published in Geneva but aimed at the French market. This was a major event in the history of the French language: the appearance in French of a major theological work. Calvin's elegant French style played an important formative role in the development of French as a modern language. This and later French editions showed Calvin's concern to reach not just the intelligentsia but also the laity.

1543 Edition

This less radical revision was published in March 1543, at Strassburg. It was nearing completion in January 1542. Thus, though it was completed in Geneva, it reflects the influence of Calvin's three years at Strassburg, which ended in September 1541. The seventeen chapters of 1539 had become twenty-one. Again there was a French translation, which appeared in 1545.

1550 Edition

This edition appeared early in 1550 at Geneva. The main new feature was the division of the chapters into sections. There was a French translation, which appeared the following year.

1559 Edition

During the winter of 1558/59 Calvin lay ill with malaria yet determined to produce a definitive edition of the *Institutes*. This appeared in September 1559, at Geneva. In this edition Calvin added more material and thoroughly rearranged the book. He tells us that though he did not regret the earlier editions, he had never been satisfied with the arrangement until this edition. This edition is about 25 percent longer than the 1550 edition. It is roughly as long as Genesis to Luke, inclusive. It now consists of eighty chapters divided among four books. The four books correspond to the four sections of the Apostles' Creed, but this is a formal arrangement, and it is wrong to see the work as an exposition of the creed. The resurrection comes at the end of book 3, far from its position in the creed. There was a French translation, which appeared in 1560. Because this appeared after the final Latin edition, some regard it as the truly definitive version, but that is to mistake the role of the French translations. The Latin is the definitive text, and the translations at times simplify it in order to make it more accessible to nonscholars.

The *Institutes* has been printed often, and in a wide variety of languages. Both the 1536 and the 1559 editions are found in the *Opera Selecta Joannis Calvini*, edited by P. Barth and W. Niesel. The 1536 edition appears in volume 1 but is not as reliable as it should be.[9] The 1559 edition appears in volumes 3 to 5.[10] This is a thoroughly reliable critical edition. The 1539 edition has been published together with a concordance.[11]

The 1536 *Institutes* has been translated into English by F. L. Battles and twice published.[12] There are four English translations of the 1559 *Institutes*: by Thomas Norton, Thomas Cranmer's son-in-law (1561);[13] by John Allen (1813);[14] by Henry Bever-

9. J. Calvin, *Opera Selecta*, ed. P. Barth (Munich: Chr. Kaiser, 1926), 1:11–283. For its inadequacies, see W. G. Hards, *A Collation of the Latin Texts of the First Edition of Calvin's Institutes* (Baltimore: [self-published at Cathedral of the Incarnation], 1958).

10. J. Calvin, *Opera Selecta*, ed. P. Barth and W. Niesel, vols. 3–5 (Munich: Chr. Kaiser, 1928, 1931, 1936, and further editions).

11. J. Calvin, *Institutes of the Christian Religion of John Calvin, 1539: Text and Concordance*, ed. R. F. Wevers (Grand Rapids: H. H. Meeter Center, 1988).

12. J. Calvin, *Institution of the Christian Religion* . . . , trans. F. L. Battles (Atlanta: John Knox Press, 1975); J. Calvin, *Institutes of the Christian Religion* . . . , trans. F. L. Battles, rev. ed. (Grand Rapids: Eerdmans with H. H. Meeter Center, 1986).

13. J. Calvin, *The Institution of Christian Religion* (London: R. Wolffe & R. Harrison, 1561), and many reprints.

14. J. Calvin, *Institutes of the Christian Religion* (London: J. Walker, J. Hatchard, 1813), and many reprints.

idge (1845);[15] and by Ford Lewis Battles (1960).[16] The last two are still in print and available electronically,[17] the latter having the advantage of a superior layout, full notes, and extensive indexes.[18]

The Purpose of the *Institutes*

Calvin's aims in preparing the successive editions of the *Institutes* can be discerned by an examination of their title pages and prefaces.

The title page of the 1536 edition is revealing:

> Embracing almost the whole sum of piety and whatever is necessary to know in the doctrine of salvation: A work most worthy to be read by all persons zealous for piety.

This was meant to be a brief summary of the Christian faith, with the goal of edification. This end is served especially by the first four chapters, modeled on the catechism. But before it appeared, there was need for another type of work. The Affair of the Placards (October 17–18, 1534) unleashed the fury of King Francis I against the French Protestants. Francis sought to justify his brutal repression on the grounds that they were seditious Anabaptists, grounds enough for most people at the time. Calvin therefore dedicated the 1536 edition to Francis as a confession of faith and as an apology for the French Protestants.

15. J. Calvin, *Institutes of the Christian Religion* (Edinburgh: Calvin Translation Society, 1845–46), and many reprints.

16. J. Calvin, *Calvin: Institutes of the Christian Religion*, ed. J. T. McNeill, trans. F. L. Battles, Library of Christian Classics 20–21 (London: SCM; Philadelphia: Westminster, 1960).

17. On the CD *John Calvin Collection* (Rio, WI: AGES Library, 1998). The CD has all the material from MB, but the pagination is different so many of the references in the present volume will be of no use.

18. There have also been a number of abridgements of the *Institutes*, such as J. Calvin, *The Institutes of Christian Religion*, ed. T. Lane and H. Osborne (London, Hodder & Stoughton, 1986; Grand Rapids: Baker, 1987), and many reprints. The passages selected for that abridgement are closely related to the readings selected in the present volume.

This purpose is seen most clearly in the "Prefatory Address" to the king; see especially pp. 9–10.[19]

In his *Letter to the Reader* at the beginning of the 1539 edition, Calvin explains how the *Institutes* should be used. It is intended as an introduction and guide to the study of Scripture and to complement his commentaries. Because of the *Institutes,* Calvin need not digress at length on doctrinal matters in his commentaries (pp. 4–5). This warns us against falling into the common error of viewing Calvin as "a man of one book"—the *Institutes.* The *Institutes* and the commentaries are designed to be used together: the *Institutes* to provide a theological undergirding for the commentaries, and the commentaries to provide a more solid exegesis of the passages cited in the *Institutes.* So when he gives a biblical reference in the *Institutes,* Calvin may be pointing not just to the biblical text itself, but also to his commentary on that passage.

The French editions from 1541 to 1551 contain an introduction titled *Subject Matter of the Present Work* (pp. 6–8). Here Calvin presents the *Institutes* as a guide to the laity in their study of the Bible. The Scriptures contain a perfect doctrine, to which nothing can be added, but the beginner needs guidance in order to study them profitably. The *Institutes* is offered for that purpose, as "a summary of Christian doctrine" and an introduction to the profitable reading of both the Old and New Testaments. The introductions to the various modern editions are also useful for background and orientation.[20]

Calvin's *Institutes* is still widely read today, more so than any other major theological work of comparable age. This is in part because of Calvin's great success in his aim of "lucid brevity": covering a topic briefly, yet expressing clearly what he had to say. This makes his writing easier to read than most comparable works. It is also in part because of his great theological skills, which are appreciated even by those who may

19. Calvin also explains why he wrote this edition in his *Commentary on Psalms,* xli–xlii ("Author's Preface").

20. A helpful account of the 1536 edition is found in T. H. L. Parker, *John Calvin* (London: J. M. Dent, 1975), chap. 3.

differ from him on particular doctrines, be that infant baptism or predestination.

The Structure of the 1559 *Institutes*

For the last century, Calvin scholars have been debating the structure of the 1559 *Institutes*, with a variety of theories about this.[21] Calvin himself gives us his own structure in the titles of the four books:

Book 1. The Knowledge of God the Creator
Book 2. The Knowledge of God the Redeemer in Christ . . .
Book 3. The Way in Which We Receive the Grace of
         Christ . . .
Book 4. The External Means or Aids by Which God Invites
         Us into the Society of Christ . . .

Scholars have developed a number of theories that propose a deeper underlying structure. Edward Dowey claimed, especially on the basis of a comment of Calvin in 1.2.1, that the basic structure of the *Institutes* is twofold: the knowledge of God as Creator and as Redeemer.[22] Indeed, he sees the break between these two as coming partway through book 2.[23] It is true that there is this division in the *Institutes*, but to take it as the fundamental division and to divide the *Institutes* in a way that is so different from Calvin's own division is implausible. More plausibly, T. H. L. Parker argued that the *Institutes* is structured according to the four articles of the Apostles' Creed.[24] This has the merit that the contents of each book do roughly match this division, but not exactly. If following the creed, book 3 should be about the Holy Spirit, who is not mentioned in Calvin's title.

21. For more on this, see Charles Partee, *The Theology of John Calvin* (Louisville: Westminster John Knox, 2008), 35–43.
22. E. A. Dowey, *The Knowledge of God in Calvin's Theology* (Grand Rapids: Eerdmans, 1951; rev. ed., 1994), 41–49 (page numbers fit the rev. ed.).
23. Ibid., 45: "Book II really begins only in chapter vi."
24. T. H. L. Parker, *Calvin's Doctrine of the Knowledge of God*, 2nd ed. (Edinburgh: Oliver & Boyd, 1969), 6.

On this schema, the final resurrection should come in book 4, whereas it actually comes at the end of book 3. So though there are indeed many parallels between the structure of the *Institutes* and that of the Apostles' Creed, if Calvin did intend to base his work upon it, one can only say that he made a bad job of it.[25] Finally, Charles Partee has proposed a twofold division between "God for Us" (books 1 and 2) and "God with Us" (books 3 and 4).[26] It is certainly true that the material fits this twofold division (as it also fits Dowey's twofold division of God as Creator and Redeemer), but that does not mean that Calvin intended either of these as his basic structure. Ultimately, it is Calvin's own structure that is normative, not the structures proposed by various scholars as underlying it.

25. The same applies even more to the suggestion of Philip Butin that the Trinity is the organizing or structural paradigm for the 1559 *Institutes*, though he does qualify this by referring to the Apostles' Creed (P. W. Butin, *Revelation, Redemption, and Response: Calvin's Trinitarian Understanding of the Divine-Human Relationship* [New York: Oxford University Press, 1995], 19, 124). A division into four books does not immediately suggest a structure based on the Trinity.

26. Partee, *Theology of Calvin*, 40–43.

Introduction to the Notes

The *Institutes* is divided into books, chapters, and sections. Thus 3.12.4 = book 3, chapter 12, section 4. (Books about Calvin sometimes use Roman numerals: III.xii.4.) In these notes, I will use the symbol § for section: §4 = section 4; §§5–6 = sections 5–6.

The *Institutes* went through five major editions, and different material was introduced by Calvin at different stages. The small letters *a–e* in MB tell you at which stage portions of the text were added. See pp. xxiv, xxvii for details. This reader's guide, however, is designed to help readers understand and appreciate the teaching of the definitive 1559 edition, not to trace material back to the different earlier editions. Only occasionally will mention be made of when material was first introduced into the *Institutes*.

The titles of the books and the chapters are from Calvin and are important. The section headings are *not* Calvin's. Some of them (e.g., 1.2.2) are followed by an asterisk or a dagger in MB. These symbols can be ignored, but see pp. xix–xx or xxvii if your curiosity gets the better of you. The titles of chapters in my notes are not usually Calvin's (which are often excessively long and ponderous) but are intended to be brief summaries of his titles.

The MB edition has many footnotes offering a wealth of information. The most significant ones are indicated in the notes below. Some readers may wish to read all of the MB footnotes, but you can safely ignore them except where either your curiosity or these notes point to them.

There is one major flaw in MB. Though it aims to be a faithful translation of Calvin's text, no such care has been taken with Calvin's references. So, when it comes to biblical references, the fact that a passage is cited in the text (in square brackets) is absolutely no guarantee that Calvin cited it or even had it in mind. By no means all of Calvin's biblical references are found in MB, and by no means all of the references found there are from Calvin. So it is totally unreliable as an indicator of Calvin's citation of Scripture. The same applies to Calvin's citation of patristic and medieval authors. There are many such marginal citations in Calvin's 1559 *Institutes*. These are (mostly) found in the footnotes to MB. Unfortunately the footnotes also contain numerous other such references not found in Calvin. So the reader has no way of knowing whether a reference to Chrysostom or Cyprian in the footnotes means that Calvin cited them or simply that the editor thought them relevant. A glance at the author index (pp. 1626–27) indicates that Thomas Aquinas is cited frequently in the footnotes. Some careless scholars have been misled by this into supposing that Calvin himself frequently referred to Thomas, while in fact Calvin names Thomas just four times in all his writings (two of these in the *Institutes*) and may never have read him.[1]

Our set reading does not include the whole of the *Institutes*. In my notes, I will give a brief indication of what we are leaving out, enclosed within square brackets [like this]. If you want more detail, you can adopt one of the strategies listed in "How to Use This Book," above.

---

1. See A. N. S. Lane, *John Calvin: Student of the Church Fathers* (Edinburgh: T&T Clark, 1999), 44–45.

READING GUIDE

1

Introductory Material
(Pp. 3–8; "Prefatory Address" §§1, 3–4, 6)

Introduction

Calvin wrote an introductory "Letter to the Reader," which is found in all of the Latin editions from 1539. In 1559 he modified part of this and added a new section. In the French editions from 1541 to 1551 was a corresponding item, and MB includes this as well.

Calvin dedicated the first edition (1536) to King Francis I of France. His "Prefatory Address" remains in all subsequent editions, with some additions. Its main purpose is to refute seven charges that had been brought against the Evangelicals.

Questions

How did Calvin see the *Institutes* relating to Scripture and to his commentaries? How does Calvin answer the charge of novelty

("Prefatory Address" §§3–4)? Where was the true church in the Middle Ages ("Prefatory Address" §6)?

Pp. 3–5. John Calvin to the Reader

As can be seen from the small letters, this 1559 text is a revision of the 1539 *Letter to the Reader*. The superscript *b* at the beginning indicates that this is from 1539; the superscript *e(b)* near the end of the paragraph indicates that the following text, from 1539 material (*b*), was revised in 1559 (*e*). At the bottom of the page, the superscript *b* indicates that what follows is from 1539. The superscript *e* near the top of the next page indicates that what follows is from 1559, until the superscript *b* at the beginning of the last paragraph on that page, and so on. See pp. xxiv and xxvii for details.

The first paragraph is very important for the history of the different editions; especially see the next-to-last sentence. The 1559 edition was the first with which Calvin was really satisfied.

The second paragraph explains the circumstances behind the preparation of the 1559 edition. Its last sentence has turned out to be truer than Calvin could have realized.

The third paragraph is not important and can be ignored.

In the fourth paragraph, Calvin explains how the *Institutes* relates to his commentaries. In line 6 of p. 5, "Scripture" should be "my commentaries."

Pp. 6–8. Subject Matter of the Present Work

This comes from the 1541–51 French editions, *not* (as MB claims) the 1560 edition.

In the first paragraph, Calvin explains the relation between the Bible and the *Institutes*.

Scripture is perfect and sufficient but not so clear that we need no help in understanding it. This is the purpose of the French *Institutes*: to guide the (non-Latin-speaking) laity toward a clearer grasp of the teaching of Scripture. The last six lines of footnote 8 are of interest.

In the second paragraph, Calvin explains his motive for translating the *Institutes* into French. He is concerned for the whole

French *nation* (line 7). Calvin again explains (as in par. 4 of the Latin "Letter to the Reader") the relation between the *Institutes* and his commentaries. Notice again, after the number for footnote 9, "the greatest possible brevity."

In the third paragraph, Calvin gives some advice about how to read the *Institutes.* You may find the third sentence an encouragement!

Prefatory Address. Footnotes 1, 8, 12, 39, 44, and 45 are of interest.

§1. Calvin explains how the 1536 edition was written. Originally it was to have been a simple handbook of doctrine. But after the affair of the Placards[1] on October 17–18, 1534, Francis launched a bitter persecution of French Protestants. This led Calvin to dedicate the work to Francis as a confession of faith.

[**§2.** The Evangelicals base their teaching on Scripture and are persecuted; the Roman clergy fight for doctrines that have no scriptural basis.]

§3. In the first paragraph, Calvin outlines seven charges brought against the Evangelicals: (1) novelty, (2) uncertainty, (3) lack of miracles, (4) rejection of the early church fathers, (5) rejection of custom, (6) schism, (7) sedition. The rest of the "Prefatory Address" is devoted to answering these charges in turn.

The second and third paragraphs answer the charge of novelty. Calvin here responds by saying that his doctrine is as old as Scripture. This is all very well, but it does not meet the following charge, brought against Calvin by Cardinal Sadolet in 1539:

> The point in dispute is, Whether [it is] more expedient for your salvation, and whether you think you will do what is more pleasing to God, by believing and following what

---

1. For details of this, see p. xxxi of MB and my introduction titled "John Calvin and His *Institutes*," above.

the Catholic Church throughout the whole world, now for more than fifteen hundred years, or (if we require clear and certain recorded notice of the facts) for more than thirteen hundred years, approves with general consent; or innovations introduced within these twenty-five years, by crafty, or, as they think themselves, acute men; but men certainly who are not themselves the Catholic Church?[2]

Such a charge requires an appeal to more than Scripture, and this Calvin provides in §4. In the fourth paragraph, Calvin answers charge 2. Charge 3 is answered in the remaining paragraphs of §3, which are less important.

§4 answers charge 4 and thereby provides a further answer to the charge of novelty. Calvin's doctrine is not "new" (a damning charge when *all* agreed that "nothing new can be true") because it is scriptural *and* because it is in line with the teaching of the early fathers, before the church went astray. Essentially Calvin makes two claims in this section: the fathers do not support the Roman Catholic position *and* by and large they do support the Reformed position. Both claims come in the first paragraph. Calvin treats the fathers with respect, but they are not infallible: they must be tested by Scripture. They made mistakes, and Calvin accuses the Roman Catholics of following these and thus gathering dung amid gold.

In the following paragraphs, Calvin, like a defense lawyer, calls the fathers as witnesses for his case. There is no need to pay attention to the details; it is the overall effect that you should grasp.

In the final paragraph of §4, Calvin is very rude about the medieval scholastic theologians. These complaints were

2. H. Beveridge, ed., *Selected Works of John Calvin: Tracts*, Calvin Translation Society (repr., Grand Rapids: Baker, 1983), 1:14, from his 1539 letter to the Genevans. These words were written some four years later than Calvin's "Prefatory Address," but they have been quoted here because they express most succinctly the charge that Calvin then had to face.

also voiced by Roman Catholic humanists, such as Erasmus in his *Praise of Folly*.[3]

[§5 answers charge 5. The appeal to custom is mistaken since the majority is not always right.]

§6 answers charge 6 (schism) and also the question of where the true church was to be found in the Middle Ages. This was (and is) an important question for Protestants to answer, as is seen from this question posed by the Roman Catholic polemicist John Eck in 1529:

> Christ is no bigamist: the Church of the apostles and ours are one Church. Before Luther was born, there was the Church that believed the Mass a sacrifice, seven sacraments, etc. She was the bride of Christ. Therefore now let us remain with that same Church, and not be joined to the Church of the wicked. Christ, because He loves the Church His bride, did not leave her, neither for five hundred nor a thousand years. How then would the Head desert His body for so long a time?[4]

This argument was especially powerful in the early years of the Reformation, when Protestantism was young and novelty was suspect.

[§7 answers charge 7. It is the Anabaptists, who at the time were occupying Münster, who are seditious. The apostles faced similar unjust accusations. §8 is Calvin's final appeal to Francis for a fair hearing and for justice. The closing date should be August 23, 1535 (n. 51).]

3. Erasmus, *Praise of Folly and Letter to Maarten van Dorp*, rev. ed. (London: Penguin, 1993), 86–95.
4. J. Eck, *Enchiridion of Commonplaces*, 1.1, trans. F. L. Battles (Grand Rapids: Baker, 1979), 8.

The Knowledge
of God the Creator

The first book focuses on knowing God and, more particularly,
God as Creator. The opening chapters consider the extent to
which, without the benefit of special revelation (also known
as Judeo-Christian revelation) people can or do know God
or know about him. After a number of short chapters on our
natural awareness of God (chaps. 1–4), there is a substantial
chapter on the revelation of God in creation (chap. 5). After
showing that nature is sufficient only to render us inexcusable,
Calvin then turns to God's revelation in Scripture and the role
of the Holy Spirit in bearing witness to it (chaps. 6–9). This
leads to an account of the true God—Father, Son, and Holy
Spirit—who is not to be confused with heathen gods and who
may not be represented by outward images (chaps. 10–13).

God is the Creator, and Calvin devotes chapters to creation in general (mainly angels and demons; chap. 14) and to humanity in particular (chap. 15). Finally, three chapters are devoted to God's providence, his sovereign rule over history (chaps. 16–18).

2

Knowing God and Ourselves
(1.1–4)

Introduction

Calvin begins by arguing that the knowledge of God and of
ourselves are interlinked: we cannot understand ourselves aright
without seeing ourselves in relation to God, and we know God
as he relates to us (chaps. 1–2). He goes on, more controversially,
to argue that there is in all people a natural awareness of God,
though this is distorted and corrupted by sin (chaps. 3–4).

Questions

Why must the knowledge of God and the knowledge of ourselves
be held together (1.1–2)? What role is played by our "natural
awareness" of God (1.3–4)?

1.1. The Knowledge of God and Ourselves. Footnotes 2, 3 (lines
1–7), 4, and 7 are of interest.
    There are two things to observe at the beginning of each
chapter of the *Institutes*: the title of the chapter (which is

by Calvin) and the opening sentence (or two), which sets the scene for the chapter.[1]

§1. The knowledge of God and of ourselves and how they are tied together. The famous opening sentence follows a long tradition (see n. 3). Knowledge of ourselves leads us to knowledge of God. Because of creation and because of sin: "we cannot seriously aspire to [God] before we begin to become displeased with ourselves." Calvin is not thinking of a merely theoretical knowledge *about* God and ourselves. He means knowing God and ourselves in a personal, "existential" way.

§2. We cannot *truly* know ourselves until we know God; only then do we appreciate our sinfulness. (Calvin strongly emphasizes human sinfulness, perhaps excessively so. In today's church, the tendency is in the other direction, so Calvin can provide a useful corrective.) The illustration of looking into the sun reminds us that Calvin is constantly giving such illustrations as his visual aids.

§3. Calvin correctly reminds us that in Scripture those who encounter God are deeply aware of their sinfulness. There are other passages he could have added.

1.2. The Knowledge of God. Footnotes 1–4 are of interest.

§1. In the first sentence Calvin defines the knowledge of God. It includes "piety," which is also defined in the last few lines of §1. Footnotes 2 and 3 are very important. In 1.2–5 we consider the knowledge of God *apart from* special revelation. Then 1.6 brings Scripture into the picture.

§2. Calvin is not interested in idle speculation about God's nature. He rejects the idea of an "idle" God, a remote God not involved in the world, as was later taught by Deism. His God is the God of providence, who controls all things (1.16–18). In the second paragraph he stresses that true knowledge of God involves the one true God and involves

---

1. For the second point, I am indebted to T. H. L. Parker, my research supervisor (oral communication).

a trusting, loving, and respectful relationship with him. Especially read the last two sentences. The final paragraph gives us a definition of true religion.

1.3. The Natural Awareness of God. Footnotes 1 and 2 are of interest.

§1. Humanity has a natural awareness of God, and this is universal. Because it is universal, we are left without excuse for our sin. Observe the parallels with Romans 1:18–32 in 1.3–5. Calvin appeals to the religiosity of primitive humanity, a controversial claim today.

§2. It is true that religion has been used to manipulate people, but this would never have succeeded had there not been a natural human awareness of God. Even atheists have a fear of God, a more plausible claim in the sixteenth century than the twenty-first.

§3. This natural awareness of God cannot be effaced. It is only the worship of God that makes us superior to the animals. §§2–3 would need to be rewritten today, when atheism is much more widespread.

1.4. Sinners Distort This Awareness of God

§1. A blistering attack on unregenerate humanity. The seeds of religion are perverted so that there is no true piety. Humanity is blind, but not thereby excused, for the blindness arises from pride and obstinacy.

§2. Further attack. The second sentence explains how a practical rejection of God leads to wrong beliefs about him. Theoretical atheism arises from practical atheism. Note also the further attack on the "idle" Deist God, who does nothing.

§3. A shrewd attack on popular/folk religion. Zeal for religion is not enough. Religion without truth is no good.

§4. Contrast between voluntary, reverent fear of God and slavish, forced fear. Also contrast between a confused knowledge of God and true piety.

3

God Revealed in Creation
(1.5.1–4, 6–15)

Introduction

God is revealed in the universe in general, especially in humanity and in providence. But this revelation is of limited value because sinful humanity suppresses and distorts it. The result is not that all people know the truth about God but rather that all are without excuse because of the way in which they have distorted it.

Questions

In what ways is God made manifest in the created order? What is the effect of this upon unregenerate humanity?

1.5. God Known through Creation and Providence. Footnotes 2, 4, 7, 11, 23, 25–27, 29, 36, and 41 are of interest.

In 1.2–5, because of the subject matter (the knowledge of God outside of special revelation), there are many references to the pagan classics. These become much less frequent from 1.6 onward, when Calvin turns to our knowledge of God through his special revelation.

God Is Revealed in the Created Universe (§§1–2)

§1. To help us to know him, God gave us a "seed of religion" and also revealed himself in creation. The first five sentences state the argument, which Calvin then supports from Scripture. At the bottom of p. 52, the reference to the mirror is a favorite analogy of Calvin's.[1]

§2. The sciences and the arts help us to perceive God, but there is more than enough for even the simplest to see. See the last sentence on the human body. The theory of evolution challenges this argument, providing an alternative explanation.

God Is to Be Seen in Humanity in Particular (§§3–6)

§3. We need only look within ourselves to find God. The last sentence of §3 introduces an idea close to Calvin's heart and central to his theology.

§4. Unfortunately, humanity suppresses this evidence in pride and ingratitude. What people would not say then (p. 56, sentence 1) is said today by the theory of evolution.

[§5 is an attack on certain pagan Greek errors.]

§6. The folly of missing God in human nature and the created universe. The fact that this folly is that much more widespread today does not prove that it is not folly. Calvin's theory (that humanity suppresses and conceals the manifestations of God) amply accounts for current refusals to acknowledge that creation points to God.

1. See W. F. Keesecker, "John Calvin's Mirror," *Theology Today* 17 (1960): 288–89.

God Is Manifest in His Ongoing Providential Rule over the Universe (§§7–10)

§7. God providentially rules society. This section might lead one to suppose that Calvin would be sympathetic to modern "prosperity doctrines": if we follow God we will certainly be prosperous and healthy. Calvin's position is far removed from this, as will be clear in his teaching on the Christian life (3.6–10). The next-to-last sentence, an idea taken up again in §10, is in the form of a quotation from Augustine.

§8. Examples from Scripture. This section is less important, but read the last sentence on p. 60.

§9. God is clearly manifested in his works, as stated in the first sentence. The next sentence deals with the nature of a true knowledge of God. The way to find God is not to speculate concerning his essence but to contemplate his works.

§10. The inequity of the treatment that we receive in this life is a clear pointer to the existence of a future life. Notice the Augustine quotation at the end of the first paragraph. The second paragraph to some extent summarizes the argument thus far: the need to see God in his works (§§7–10) but more especially in ourselves (§§3–6).

This Evidence Is of No Profit Because Humanity Goes Astray (§§11–12)

§11. Notice the first sentence and then the third sentence on p. 64. In paragraph 2, we see how the philosophers have gone astray, although providence is so manifest.

§12. How humanity has gone astray. The second paragraph is less important, but see the last sentence, the conclusion to §§11–12.

Because We Distort the Manifest Revelation of God, We Are without Excuse (§§13–15)

§13. Read the first and last sentences of the second paragraph.

§14. There is no true knowledge of God derived from nature alone. But since God is in fact manifest in nature, we are without excuse. Here, as in much of 1.5, Calvin follows Romans 1:18–32.

§15. Again, there is no excuse.

4

The Bible and the Holy Spirit
(1.6–7; 1.8.1, 13; 1.9)

Introduction

Because sinful humanity suppresses and distorts the revelation of God in creation, a clearer revelation is needed, and this is found in Scripture (chap. 6). But how can we be *sure* that it is from God? The answer lies in the witness that the Holy Spirit bears to Scripture (chap. 7). This witness of the Spirit remains primary, though it can be supplemented by rational apologetic arguments (chap. 8). Some Radicals were claiming special revelations of the Spirit independently of Scripture, which led them to despise Scripture. Calvin responds that the Holy Spirit who inspired Scripture will not teach us to despise or contradict it (chap. 9).

Questions

Why do we need the Bible (1.6)? How does the Spirit bear witness to the Word, and what part does rational argument play in this (1.7–8)? How should we react to alleged manifestations of the Holy Spirit (1.9)?

1.6. Need for Scripture to Come to God

§1. The first sentence (which in the Latin begins with "Therefore") gives us the conclusion of 1.5. But while God is so manifest in creation (sent. 1), we need more (sent. 2). This "more" is Scripture (sent. 3). Calvin very aptly compares the role of Scripture here to the help provided by spectacles.

In the second paragraph Calvin distinguishes two stages in the knowledge of God: to know him as *Creator* (the theme of bk. 1) and to know him as *Redeemer* (the theme of bks. 2–4). In book 1 he confines himself largely to God as Creator, with passing references to salvation. In 1.1–5 he considered it primarily without reference to Scripture; in 1.6–18 he considers it in the light of Scripture.

§2. The importance of Scripture and our need to study it. Calvin refers to the world as a theater, even before Shakespeare's "All the world's a stage."

§3. More on the inadequacy of revelation in nature and the need for Scripture if we are not to lose our way. The analogy of the labyrinth is one of Calvin's favorite, which we have already met in 1.5.12 (n. 36).[1]

§4. Quotations from the Psalms.

1.7. The Witness of the Spirit to Scripture's Authority. Footnote 18 is of interest.

---

1. For an imaginative account of the labyrinth's significance as a key to Calvin's personality, cf. W. J. Bouwsma, *John Calvin: A Sixteenth-Century Portrait* (New York: Oxford University Press, 1988), esp. 45–48. For a critique of this, see Muller, *Unaccommodated Calvin*, 79–98.

§1. Calvin's aim is to "banish all doubt" (sent. 1). God does not daily speak from heaven (sent. 3), but we need to come to see the Scriptures as *God's* words (sent. 4).

In paragraph 2, Calvin poses two distinct questions: How can we know that the Scriptures are from God? How can we know which books belong in the Bible, in the canon of Scripture? This chapter gives an important answer to the first question (which is no less relevant today than in Calvin's time) but never really tackles the second question.

Calvin faced Roman Catholic claims that the *church* bestows authority on Scripture and that we need to turn to the church for conviction on this matter. In the last three sentences, he accuses Rome of thereby basing scriptural authority on *human* judgment. But for Roman Catholics the church is a *divine* institution, appointed by God. We have here a fundamental difference between Rome and the Reformation.

Calvin expresses his concern at the end of the paragraph: "What will happen to miserable consciences seeking firm assurance of eternal life if all promises of it consist in and depend solely upon the judgment of men?" The reason why we need to be sure about Scripture is not so that we can speculate about theology, but so as to provide the basis for trusting God's promises for our salvation, as Calvin will argue in 3.2 on saving faith.

§2. Calvin responds with the argument that the church is itself based on Scripture. He is a little too slick here and glides too easily from the priority of the apostolic *teaching* (which gave birth to the church) to the priority of the apostolic *writings*. It cannot be denied that the church predates the New Testament writings by at least twenty years *and* that the New Testament canon was defined by the Catholic Church. Calvin is on surer ground in the second half of §2 (from p. 76, line 6). Here he *qualifies,* rather than *denies,* the role of the church. It is true that the church gives the seal of approval to the Scriptures both in the definition of the canon and in ongoing witness to Scripture. But the church is not thereby *giving* the Scriptures authority. Instead, it is acknowledging and pointing to what is clear to all who have eyes to see. (Similarly, when the church declares that Jesus is the Son of God, it is recognizing that fact, not *making* him Son of God.) See especially the last sentence. The problem is not that the Bible does not bear evident marks of being God's Word, but rather that our sin blinds us and keeps us from seeing the obvious. The role of the Holy Spirit is not to whisper in our ears that the Bible is God's Word but to open our eyes to see what is self-evident.

§3. Controversy over a passage from Augustine. This section is less important but not without interest. The quotation (first sentence) was possibly the most debated nonbiblical sentence in the sixteenth century. Calvin interprets it to refer to the (undoubted) apologetic function of the church in pointing unbelievers to the Scriptures. In the second paragraph, he argues that believers ought to seek the foundation for their certainty elsewhere—from the witness of the Holy Spirit.

§4. Notice the first two sentences. Arguments for the authority of Scripture have some value but do not suffice. If we are to have the certainty that we need, we require the "secret testimony of the Spirit" (sentence before footnote 12). In paragraph 2, we see why arguments do not suffice (see the first sentence). Arguments give birth to probable opinions, not to the certainty of faith. In the section after footnote 14, especially observe the reference to Isaiah, which gives us the heart of Calvin's case. Until the Spirit illumines our minds, we ever waver among many doubts (last sentence).

§5. The first half of the first paragraph is also a very important summary of Calvin's case. When the Spirit seals Scripture upon our hearts, we see that it is self-evidently God's Word. In the second half of the second paragraph (after Isa. 43:10), Calvin claims that *each believer* experiences this within himself. Does this mean that anyone who doubts that the Bible is God's Word does not have God's Spirit? No. Calvin was both pastorally sensitive and realistic. He acknowledges elsewhere that our faith is *always* such that we have to pray, "Lord, help my unbelief" (cf. Mark 9:24). If we have doubts, the conclusion is not that we do not have God's Spirit, but rather that we ought to be more open to his witness to God's Word and more ready to heed it.

The third paragraph is less important. The final sentence points forward to doctrines yet to come.

1.8. Proofs That Establish the Credibility of Scripture—as far as human reason goes.

The opening and concluding lines of 1.8 set out again the relation between such "proofs" and the inner witness of the Spirit. The remainder of the chapter (not part of the designated reading) gives us Calvin's apologetic for the truth of Scripture. Many, but not all, of Calvin's "proofs" are now out of date by virtue of the fact that he lived before the rise of biblical criticism. But this does not matter, because modern apologists have supplied many other arguments to take their place. Yet Calvin's perceptive comments on the relation between such proofs and the certainty of faith are *not* out of date.

§1. Only the first three sentences need be read. Rational proofs or the testimony of the church cannot produce the certainty of faith. This requires the foundation of the witness of the Spirit. But once we have that foundation, other arguments are helpful.

§13. Only the last paragraph need be read. The same points as in §1 are repeated. Human testimonies, such as rational proofs, are "secondary aids to our feebleness."

1.9. The Relation between God's Word and God's Spirit

§1. The first two sentences set out the problem: people claiming to know better about God than the Scriptures. This is as much an issue today as in Calvin's time. Liberal theologians reject the teaching of Scripture on the grounds that it is contrary to "the Spirit of Christ," whatever that may be.[2] Others are claiming new revelations that add to the biblical revelation. Calvin argues that there is no other Holy Spirit than the one who inspired the Scriptures, and the Spirit does not contradict himself. To be open to the Holy Spirit means (among other things) to be receptive to the Scriptures, which he inspired. The last sentence summarizes Calvin's position.

§2. Any alleged manifestation of the Spirit today should be tested by the Word of God.

§3. The unity of the Word and the Spirit. Note especially the second half of paragraph 1. The Holy Spirit works only where the Word of God is honored. Experience in recent years would confirm this claim. Again, the Word of God is confirmed to us by the Holy Spirit (1.7). The sentence beginning "For by a kind of mutual bond . . ." supplies an important summary.

In the second paragraph, Calvin appears to identify the "prophecies" of 1 Thessalonians 5:20 with Scripture. In his commentary on that verse, he identifies prophecy with biblical exposition—which was certainly wrong for Paul's day and is not adequate for today. The phenomenon of prophecy today makes this chapter *more* rather than less relevant. It makes all the more urgent the need to test all alleged prophecies by Scripture (1 Cor. 14:29; 1 Thess. 5:20–21). Calvin's stress on the unity of Word and Spirit is a powerful safeguard against false prophecies. There are sects around today that began as orthodox Christian groups but went off the rails by accepting "new revelations." See the final sentence of the chapter.

The teaching of this chapter is nicely captured by two recent epigrams:

2. E.g., G. Lampe, *God as Spirit* (Oxford: Oxford University Press, 1977; London: SCM, 1983), 113, where it is stated that the "Christ-Spirit" leads us to reject the historical Jesus's teaching on hell, as recorded in the Gospels.

The Spirit without the Word is dangerous;
the Word without the Spirit is deadly;
the Word with the Spirit is dynamite.

And more succinctly:

Too much Word—dry up;
too much Spirit—blow up;
Word and Spirit—grow up.

5

Idolatry and the Trinity
(1.11.1–5, 12; 1.13.2–3, 6–7, 16–20)

Introduction

Reformed Protestantism was strongly opposed to all forms of idolatry. Heathen gods are not to be confused with the true God (chap. 10). Nor is the true God to be represented by visible images (chap. 11). And the worship of God is not compatible with the worship or veneration of saints (chap. 12). Having removed these obstacles, Calvin turns to the exposition of the orthodox doctrine of the Trinity, as taught by the early fathers (chap. 13).

Questions

What is Calvin's attitude toward images of God (1.11)? How does Calvin relate together the oneness and the threeness of God (1.13)?

[1.10. The True God versus Heathen Gods. God reveals himself in his creation (1.5), and there is a widespread awareness of monotheism, but Scripture rejects all the gods of the heathen.]

1.11. Making Images of God Is Unlawful. Footnotes 1 and 10 are of interest.

§1. To represent God by an outward form is to corrupt his glory. This is why the second commandment outlaws such images. God repudiates all images of himself.

§2. Further scriptural proof. To seek a visible form of God is to depart from him. Images displease God because they dishonor his majesty.

§3. Attempts to justify images from Scripture are refuted. See the last sentence.

§4. Scripture teaches us that "all we conceive concerning God in our minds is an insipid fiction." Calvin quotes from the pagan writer Horace's satires against idolatry and the prophet Isaiah's similar satire. In the second paragraph Calvin attacks the Eastern Orthodox practice of representing God with icons. Read the last sentence.

§5. Calvin attacks Gregory the Great's description of images as the books of the unlearned. Such images in fact misrepresent God. See the last sentence.

[Calvin appeals to antiquity in §6. Roman Catholic images are grossly indecent. The cure for the unlearned is not images but proper teaching (§7). Images arise from fallen human nature (§8). It is no excuse to claim to worship God *in* the idol, a pagan claim taken over by Roman Catholics (§9). Contemporary Roman Catholic practice is simply idolatry (§10). It is no excuse to claim that images are given "service" but not "worship" (§11).]

§12. Calvin does not prohibit *all* images, only images *of* God.

[Calvin appeals to a pure antiquity (§13) and attacks the Second Council of Nicaea (AD 787), which approved the worship of images (§§14–16).]

[1.12. God Alone Is to Be Worshiped, not lesser deities or saints. The distinction between "service" (of the saints) and "worship" (of God) is spurious (see 1.11.11). It is sacrilege to offer any form of worship to anyone other than God alone (§3).]

1.13. The One Essence of God Contains Three Persons. Footnotes 5, 7a, 36, 41, and 43 are of interest.

[§1 refutes wrong ideas about God, including the idea that God has literal eyes, ears, and so forth. At the end, see the famous statement that in speaking to us, God babbles to us just as nursing mothers commonly do with their babies. In his revelation God accommodates the knowledge of himself to our slight capacity.[1]]

§2. God is one single essence in three persons/hypostases. The important point is God's threeness, not which word we use (person, etc.). In §§2–3 Calvin responds to antitrinitarians of his own time, who are listed in footnote 5.

§3. Some object to the use of nonscriptural terms here, but there is nothing wrong with using such terms if the aim is simply to explain scriptural teaching. A sparing and modest use of nonscriptural terms (such as "Trinity") is all right.

[§§4–5 further defend such terms, with reference to early church history. Calvin does not want to "battle doggedly over mere words." In the first sentence of p. 126, we have a concise summary of Calvin's doctrine of the Trinity.]

§6. Calvin defines "person" and then proceeds to explain his definition.

1. On the idea of accommodation in Calvin, see J. Balserak, *Divinity Compromised: A Study of Divine Accommodation in the Thought of John Calvin* (Dordrecht: Springer, 2006).

§7. Calvin presents a biblical argument for the deity of Christ.

[§§8–15 present biblical evidence for the deity of Christ (§§8–13) and the Spirit (§§14–15).]

§16. Father, Son, and Holy Spirit are one God.

§17. Scripture shows us that the three persons are distinct, not divided.

§18. Calvin seeks to show from Scripture the distinctions between the three persons. There is an order among them, though not a *temporal* order.

§19. These distinctions do not alter the fact of the unity of God's essence.

§20. The first sentence emphasizes soberness, brevity, and usefulness. Calvin proceeds to a brief summary of his teaching. The second paragraph is less important.

[In §21 Calvin attacks speculation. We should "conceive [God] to be as he reveals himself to us, without inquiring about him elsewhere than from his Word." In §§22–29 Calvin responds to the antitrinitarian teaching of Servetus and others.]

6

The Created World
and Humanity as Created
(1.14.13–18, 20–22; 1.15.1–4, 7–8)

Introduction

Chapter 14 describes God's creation, but seventeen of the twenty-two sections are devoted to angels and demons, the physical universe receiving only cursory treatment. A fuller treatment is given to humanity as originally created, the condition from which we fell (chap. 15).

Questions

How does Calvin view our struggle against Satan (1.14)? Why is it so important to distinguish between human nature as created/fallen (1.15)? How does Calvin understand the image of God?

1.14. God and Creation. Footnotes 28 and 30 are of interest.

[§1. We should beware speculation and keep to the scriptural account of creation. §2. The six days of creation. §§3–12 concern the angels. Calvin keeps to biblical teaching, with a stern warning against speculation (§4). Angels are not to be worshiped (§10) and do not mediate between us and the one Mediator, Jesus Christ (§12).]

§§13–19 concern devils/demons.

§13. Observe the practical concern in sentence 1. We are engaged in a lifelong struggle against a dangerous and relentless enemy.

§14. The enemy is numerous.

§15. Satan is opposed to God and to our good. There is therefore no room for peace or a truce with him.

§16. Satan is a good creature of God who has gone astray (par. 1). Scripture tells us little more than this, because it is *not necessary*. Here again, we must resist the temptation to speculate beyond what is revealed (par. 2).

§17. Satan is under God's control and does only what God wants him to do. This claim is further spelled out and defended in 1.16–18.

§18. We are on the winning side! Satan may be able to make us fall from time to time, but he will not win a *final* victory over us.

[In §19, Calvin rejects the psychological interpretation of Satan, which allows him no objective existence—a view more popular now than in Calvin's time.]

§20. Observe the delight in creation in the first sentence. Sentence 2 tells us how we are to study creation. We are to remember how God *created* all things and *preserves* them.

§21. How should we contemplate creation? Note the rule in the first sentence on p. 181. The first part is explained in the remainder of §21, the second part in §22.

§22. The second part of the rule is spelled out in sentence 2. We need to recognize that God is worthy of our trust. See also the last sentence.

1.15. Humanity as Created. Footnotes 1, 8, and 13 are of interest.

§1. Our knowledge of ourselves is twofold: as created and as fallen (sent. 2). This distinction is of *vital importance*. Non-Christians fail to see it and thus err (§§7–8). Unfortunately, so do many Christians today. If we are to understand aright the state of *fallen* humanity, we must understand how God *created* us. Otherwise the blemishes of fallen human nature are blamed upon the Creator.

§2. Humanity is composed of body and (immortal) soul. Calvin is more dualist/Platonist here than most scholars now understand the New Testament to be. His definition of the soul appears in the second sentence. Calvin offers proofs from nature and from Scripture.

§3. The image of God in humanity lies in the soul (par. 1). "Image" and "likeness" in Genesis 1:26 are synonyms, not separate entities.

§4. The original image is best seen by looking at its re-creation by Christ. The image is "frightfully deformed" by the fall, but *not* completely lost. Read especially the last two sentences of paragraph 3.

[§5. The soul is created by God and is not an emanation from his substance. §6 treats some philosophical views of the soul, mainly mistaken.]

§7. The philosophers err because they fail to distinguish between humanity as created and fallen (cf. §1). Calvin sees two basic faculties in the soul: understanding and will. The will basically follows the understanding, though not inevitably doing so, hence the fall (§8).

§8. Adam was created free and fell solely by his own choice. The fault was his alone.[1] But see the reference to pre-

---

1. Calvin, following Paul (Rom. 5:12–21), traces the fall of the human race back to Adam's sin alone, not to Eve's.

destination in paragraph 2, to be pursued in 3.23.7–8. Humanity had free will *then* (before the fall), but not *now* (par. 3). The philosophers (and some theologians) err here. Calvin at the end defends God from responsibility for the fall.

7

God's Sovereign Providence
(1.16; 1.17.1–11)

Introduction

God did not simply create the world and leave it to its devices; instead, he is the sovereign Lord who determines all that happens (chap. 16). This doctrine is given to us not for speculation but for its practical benefit in daily living (chap. 17). Though God purposes that evil events take place, he is not himself the author of evil (chap. 18).

Questions

Does God's providence leave any room for chance or uncertainty (1.16)? What are the practical benefits of the doctrine of providence (1.17)?

1.16. God Maintains and Rules the World by His Providence.
Footnotes 1, 5, and 11 are of interest.

§1. God is more than the momentary Creator of the world; he is also its ruler. Calvin contrasts two views. The "carnal" view stops with the idea of creation (second half of par. 1). Faith goes on to see God's providential rule (par. 2, especially the first sentence). Especially notice the last sentence. Calvin is concerned not with philosophical theories about determinism and sovereignty, but with God's special care and fatherly favor for his people.

§2. Providence is contrary to mere "fortune" or "chance." Carnal reason sees all as chance. Christ teaches us that "all events are governed by God's secret plan." The second paragraph, on the sun, is less important and can be omitted.

§3. God's omnipotence is more than theoretical or potential and consists in his actual rule of history (esp. sentence 3). The last clause of paragraph 1 (after footnote 6) reminds us that for Calvin this is a supremely *practical* doctrine. In the second paragraph Calvin argues that God's rule cannot be limited to his establishment of the "laws of nature" (not Calvin's term), especially for the reason given in sentence 4. The third paragraph spells out some of the benefits of this doctrine, to be developed in the next chapter. The final paragraph attacks astrology—still relevant in this age of horoscopes. We should, as the saying goes, "fear God and dread nought."[1] Note the last sentence.

§4. See especially the first sentence, in which the word "keys" should read "helm." God does not idly (note the recurrence of this word) foreknow events but directs history like a helmsman steering a boat (par. 1). In the other paragraphs Calvin contrasts two views of providence. Universal/general providence is his maintenance of the "laws of nature." This view is correct as far as it goes, but to limit God to this is wrong because it "deprives him of his control." Read

---

1. This was the motto adopted by Admiral John Arbuthnot Fisher on becoming Baron Fisher of Kilverstone. It is based on the name of *HMS Dreadnought*, the first modern battleship.

the first sentence on p. 203. Special providence, denied by carnal reason, is his control over individual events such that "nothing takes place by chance" (last sentence).

§§5–7 set out some of the scriptural support for this doctrine. These sections are less important and may be read quickly. The conclusion is in the final sentence.

§8. Providence is not to be confused with "fate." In the fifth sentence Calvin rejects a Stoic view that is akin to modern physical determinism. In the next sentence (the last of par. 1) he gives what is in effect a succinct definition of providence. The second paragraph concerns Augustine's use of the terms "fortune" and "chance." This paragraph is less important and can be omitted.

§9. From God's perspective there is no chance; but from our perspective the term is meaningful. (Tossing coins gives us a random result.) These two aspects are spelled out in the last two sentences of paragraph 1. The second and third paragraphs are less important and can be read quickly or omitted. But see the first two lines of p. 210.

1.17. How to Apply This Doctrine for Our Benefit. Footnotes 2–4, 7, and 10 are of interest.

This doctrine was for Calvin not a question of theological or philosophical speculation but the basis for practical Christian living.

§1. Paragraph 1 introduces the practical dimension. In paragraph 2, Calvin mentions "three things." These are taken up in §§3–5, in §9, and in §§6–8 and 10–11, respectively. In the rest of the paragraph, observe the need for *faith* when God's control is far from evident. In paragraph 3, this attitude is described as "moderation"—not presuming to call God to account but being willing to leave things in his hands. The last sentence sums it up.

§2. Calvin raises the issue of God's "two wills": his revealed will and his secret or hidden will, which he discusses further in 1.18.3.

§3. Paragraph 1: providence does not absolve us of responsibility for our deeds. Paragraph 2: providence does not remove the need to take precautions or to pray.

§4. Further on the issue of precautions. God's providence works *through means*, and he expects us to make use of them. Note the last two sentences. In 1567, Geneva was threatened by a large Spanish army, and the city council resolved to commit their cause to God and double the watch. Cromwell famously called on his troops to trust God and keep their powder dry. This dual response is not, as non-Christian historians have sometimes thought, evidence of lack of faith, but is thoroughly principled and in line with the approach adopted by Nehemiah (Neh. 4:9).

§5. Further on the issue of responsibility. Those who act against God's commandments may be fulfilling his purposes, but they are nonetheless guilty of sin.

§6. The benefit of the doctrine. See the second sentence. The issue of the relation between the principal cause (God) and secondary causes is taken up in §9. God cares for humanity in general and for the church in particular (§6). This affects us in prosperity (§7) and in adversity (§8), so that we need never worry (§§10–11).

§7. Prosperity. Paragraph 1 gives examples of God prospering his people. Paragraph 2 shows how we should react to this. Read especially the first sentence: gratitude for the good (§7), patience in adversity (§8), and freedom from worry (§§10–11).

§8. Adversity should be seen as sent by God, as in the biblical examples. Calvin correctly observes that this belief will profoundly affect our attitude toward suffering. Carefully read the last two sentences of the first paragraph (after "[Ps. 39:9 p.]"). Paragraphs 2 and 3 are less important and can be read quickly or omitted.

§9. An important section on the place of secondary/intermediate causes. Calvin is not saying that God causes everything *directly*. Sometimes he works through an intermediary, sometimes without one, and sometimes contrary to every intermediary (§1 presents the second of the "three things"). In general, God works by means of the regular "laws of nature" and by means of the voluntary choices of human beings. When God uses the wicked, "we must not suppose that there is a violent compulsion, as if God dragged them against their will; but in a wonderful and inconceivable manner he regulates all the movements of men, so that they still have the exercise of their will."[2]

This means that when we receive a gift, we will thank God *and* the human donor. Likewise, adversity is accepted as from God, but human agents are not excused from responsibility (par. 1). Similarly, we will not neglect secondary causes in the form of means, but nor will we put all our trust in them (par. 2). Those with a full bank account must not rely upon it in such a way as to suppose that they no longer need God. Those whose account is empty should not imagine that they are without support. Our confidence "will not so rely upon outward supports as to repose with assurance in them if they are present, or, if they are lacking, to tremble as if left destitute."

§10. Calvin graphically portrays the dangers that face us in life. These may not be quite so severe today, but the general point remains valid. Disaster threatens us at all times, it regularly strikes those around us, and in due course it will strike us, in the form of death if in no other way. How should we react to the uncertainties of life? The answer is in §11.

§11. Calvin offers us a life free not only from extreme anxiety but also from "every care" (first sentence). How? By recognizing that "nothing can befall except [God] determine it." We do not live in a random world, but in a world run by our heavenly Father. This does *not* mean that tragedy will not strike. But it does mean that it will not come unless

---

2. J. Calvin, *Commentary on the Book of the Prophet Isaiah*, trans. W. Pringle (Grand Rapids: Eerdmans, 1948), 1:352 (on Isa. 10:15).

God sends it, for our good. The second paragraph provides scriptural support and reminds us that "the devil and his crew" can do only what God wants. The third paragraph continues this point. It is less important and may be read quickly or omitted.

[§§12–14 tackle the biblical passages that talk of God "repenting." This is seen as accommodation to our weakness. Scripture teaches God's changelessness, which is to be taken literally. The "repentance" passages are to be seen as anthropomorphic.]

[1.18. God Uses the Ungodly While Remaining Pure. §§1–2 consider whether God merely permits what happens and concludes to the contrary. Here Calvin is opposed to Augustine but is following the line taken by a number of late-medieval Augustinians, as well as by Luther and Zwingli. If all things happen because they are positively ordained by God, it follows, as Calvin argues in 3.23, that God positively ordains the fall of Adam and the damnation of the reprobate. §3 answers the objection that God appears to have *two wills* (see on 1.17.2). To our feeble minds, God's will appears divided, but in fact it is one and simple in him. §4 answers the objection that Calvin makes God the author of evil, because all that happens is positively willed by him. Calvin distinguishes again between what God *commands* (in the law) and what he *ordains* (in providence), basing this on Scripture.]

The Knowledge of God the Redeemer in Christ

First Disclosed to the Fathers under the Law
and Then to Us in the Gospel

The second book turns from God as Creator to God as Redeemer, focusing on the objective work of Christ for our salvation, leaving its personal and corporate appropriation to books 3 and 4, respectively. But before turning to redemption, Calvin first explains why it is needed: because of Adam's fall and our resulting bondage to sin (chaps. 1–3). Because of this bondage, we are totally dependent upon the work of the Holy Spirit to convert us to Christ (chaps. 3–5). Salvation is in Christ alone, and the law points to him (chaps. 6–7). After a long chapter expounding the moral law as set out in the Ten Commandments (chap. 8), Calvin explains how there is both continuity and discontinuity (mainly the former) between Old and New Testaments (chaps. 9–11). The remaining chapters expound the person (chaps. 12–14) and work (chaps. 15–17) of Christ.

8

Original Sin
(2.1.1–3, 6, 8–10; 2.2.7, 12, 15, 18, 22; 2.3.3–5)

Introduction

Human nature is flawed by sin, and this is because of Adam's fall, not because it was created sinful (chap. 1). We do not have free will in the sense of being able to do the good, though we are not constrained from outside ourselves. Human reason is capable of great achievements in the secular realm but cannot grasp spiritual realities (chap. 2). Fallen human beings are the willing slaves of sin (chap. 3).

Questions

How does the fall of Adam affect us (2.1)? Of what good is fallen human reason or will capable (2.2–3)?

2.1. The Effects of Adam's Fall: Original Sin. Footnotes 1, 3, 15, and 16 are of interest.

§1. The philosophers rightly stressed the importance of knowing oneself (par. 1), but they encourage us to do this in a way that leads only to pride (par. 2). This is because they failed to grasp the basic distinction between humanity as created and as fallen (par. 3), as already expounded in 1.15.1, 7, and 8. Once we realize the position from which we have fallen, we have both humility and the desire to return (par. 4).

§2. By nature, we all love to be flattered and to have a high opinion of ourselves (par. 1). Those who praise human nature are popular, but such flattery deceives and leads folks to destruction (par. 2).

§3. *How* can we know ourselves aright? By testing ourselves against *God's* standards, which show us our sinfulness (par. 1). When we consider how God created humanity, it will arouse humility in us (par. 2). There are two parts to the knowledge of ourselves: to know what we were created for and therefore what our duties are, and to recognize our present lack of ability (par. 3).

[§4 examines the essence of Adam's sin: basically unbelief leading to ambition, pride, ingratitude, and disobedience. As a result of the fall, we are all born "infected with the contagion of sin" (§5).]

§6. See the first sentence and the third: human nature is tainted by the fall. This is explained further, culminating in the last two sentences of paragraph 2. In paragraph 3 (esp. the second sentence) Calvin stresses that human nature is sinful as *fallen*, not as God created it.

[In §7 Calvin argues that Adam's fall affects us all, not just Adam himself.]

§8. In the third sentence, Calvin offers a definition of original sin. In the second paragraph he explains that because of the fall, we all have a corrupted nature and are *therefore* guilty before God. It is not that we are guilty of Adam's sin (as Augustine held), but rather that we (including infants) are guilty because of our sinful and corrupted nature. In the third paragraph he reminds us of the amazing fertility of sin. Original sin can be called "concupiscence," a theological Latinism that basically means "lust." Like "lust," it refers especially, but by no means exclusively, to sexual desire.

§9. Sin affects the *whole* of human nature. No part is exempt. (This is what is meant by the (unfortunate) term "total depravity": not that humanity is as bad as possible, but that no part of our nature (e.g., our reason) is exempt from the taint of sin.)

§10. In the first paragraph Calvin again reminds us that it is *fallen* nature that is corrupt. The Creator is not to be blamed. The second paragraph can be omitted.

[§11 repeats that it is fallen nature, not created nature, that is sinful.]

2.2. The Bondage of the Will. Footnotes 53, 63, and 64 are of interest.

[In §1, Calvin emphasizes the importance of holding a realistic view of the freedom of the will. Self-deception profits no one. In §§2–3, he criticizes the philosophers for believing in it, and in §§4–5, he criticizes the early fathers for conceding too much to the philosophers. In §6, he is critical of the fathers and the medievals for their idea of "cooperation with grace." Only Augustine meets with approval.]

§7. Humanity does have free will in the sense outlined in sentence 1: we are "willing slaves." It is all right, like Augustine, to use the term "free will" in that sense, but Calvin considers it too grand a term for such a limited power and fears that it will immediately be misunderstood in the way that he describes in the middle of the page.

[§8. Augustine uses the term "free will" in this limited way. Read the last paragraph, where Calvin explains Augustine's usage of "free will" and gives reluctant permission to those who wish to use the term in that sense. §9 contains more of the fathers. In §§10–11, Calvin shows the dangers of a high view of free will and the importance of humility in this matter. Read the first three sentences of §10 on this.]

§12. According to the first sentence, the fall results in the corruption of humanity's natural gifts and the loss of their supernatural gifts. This is explained in paragraph 1. What is lost in Adam is restored in Christ. As a natural gift, reason is corrupted but not lost (par. 2). Similarly the will (par. 3). Unregenerate humanity has a desire for the truth but cannot find it (par. 5), especially because of curiosity (par. 6)—a very medieval point.

[In §§13–14, Calvin considers the power of natural reason in earthly matters. Read the first paragraph of §13, which introduces the subject by distinguishing between "earthly" and "heavenly" things. Calvin goes on to consider politics (§13) and the liberal and manual arts (§14).]

§15. We must recognize the truth that we see in secular writers as coming from the Holy Spirit. The Lord has left many gifts to sinful humanity, and there is much to admire in what unbelievers have taught us about earthly matters.

[This point is repeated in §§16–17. The Lord wants to teach us about earthly matters through ungodly people. To refuse to learn from them is culpable sloth (§16). These matters show that reason is innate to humanity. There is a "general" or "common" grace of God, which is given outside of the church. We also see here "some remaining traces of the image of God" (§17).]

§18. How much can the unregenerate know of spiritual/heavenly things? The first part, to footnote 66, is important. On the rest of the page, Calvin gives the superb illustration of the lightning flash, which makes his point so clearly. The last sentence sums it all up.

[§19 gives scriptural proof for the claim that "man's keenness of mind is mere blindness as far as the knowledge of God is concerned." In §20, he proceeds to argue that "man's mind can become spiritually wise only in so far as God illumines it." Similarly, in §21, "wherever the Spirit does not cast his light, all is darkness."]

§22. Calvin considers the third aspect mentioned at the beginning of §18: sinful humanity's grasp of right and wrong—in other words, "natural law," the ethical understanding that people can reach without God's special revelation. In the first paragraph, he admits that humanity has by nature some idea of right and wrong. But in paragraph 2, he characteristically argues that its purpose is simply to remove all excuse. Notice the first two sentences on p. 282, especially the second, which defines natural law.

[§23 identifies the limitations of natural law. Read the first paragraph, which is only too true of all of us at times. §24 shows that by the test of God's revealed law, natural law is seen to be defective. It is especially defective where the "first table" of the law is concerned: our relation to God. It is even defective where the "second table" is concerned: our relation to our fellow humans. The unregenerate generally approve of revenge, for example. In §25, Calvin argues that we need the Holy Spirit's help if we are to make the right ethical decisions. In §§26–27, he shows that the unregenerate cannot will the good. "There is no man[1] to whom eternal blessedness is not pleasing, yet no man aspires to it except by the impulsion of the Holy Spirit" (§26). Without the Holy Spirit, no one wills the good (§27).]

2.3. The Corruption of Human Nature and Its Fruits. Footnotes 5 and 13 are of interest.

[§1. The whole of fallen human nature is carnal until we are born again of the Spirit. §2. Romans 3 confirms this. "It is futile to seek anything good in our nature."]

§3. What of the virtuous pagan? God's grace can inwardly *restrain* those whom it does not *cleanse*. See the sentence

---

1. In MB, as in traditional English and much contemporary English, *man* is often used in the sense of human being or of humanity in general.

after "[Rom. 3:10–18]." Also read the last sentence. Calvin returns to this topic in 3.14, on the merit of works.

§4. There remains the difference between good and bad pagans. But outward virtue is not meritorious where the will is perverse (par. 1). God also bestows special gifts on some of the ungodly (par. 2). See especially p. 294, lines 9–14, plus the last sentence. Do you agree?

§5. A crucial section. Check the first sentence. The fall leads to a necessity of sinning. Fallen humanity has lost not the *will* but a *good* will (par. 1). In paragraph 2, Calvin makes the vital distinction between necessity and compulsion (better, "coercion"). The examples of God and Satan show its validity. Paragraph 3 is a good summary of Calvin's position. In the final paragraph, Calvin quotes some apt words of Bernard of Clairvaux. Humanity is under a "voluntary necessity." We are willing slaves of sin.

9

How God Works
in the Human Heart
(2.3.6–7, 10–11; 2.5.1–7, 14–15)

Introduction

Conversion, the Christian life, and perseverance to the end are all wholly the work of God's grace (chap. 3). The sovereignty of God does not preclude the genuine agency of Satan and human beings (chap. 4). Those who raise objections against this doctrine are mistaken (chap. 5).

Question

What role, if any, does Calvin leave to human beings in conversion, in the Christian life, and in perseverance to the end?

2.3. The Corruption of Human Nature and Its Fruits (cont.).
The corruption of human nature implies our total de-

pendence on God's grace. Footnotes 27, 31, and 32 are
of interest.

§6. Conversion and the Christian life are totally the work of
God. Read the third and fourth sentences on p. 297 and
the first on p. 298. In conversion, the old will is obliterated
and a new will is created. But lines 10–14 of the second
paragraph give an important qualification of this mislead-
ing language. Calvin means not the destruction of the will
but the radical change of an evil will into a good will.

§7. Calvin does not like the Catholic idea of "cooperation
with grace" because it seems to allow an independent role
to our will. God is wholly, not just partly, the author of
our good works. Calvin returns to cooperation with grace
in §§11–12.

[In §§8–9, Calvin appeals to Scripture. The last six and a half
lines of §9 summarize his argument.]

§10. See the first sentence. Calvin opposes the view (later
called Arminian) that God's grace works on us in such a
way as to make our conversion *possible* but not *inevitable*.
Calvin rejects this view, appealing to Augustine and to
Scripture. Conversion is *entirely* of God's grace.

§11. Read the first sentence. Perseverance is also wholly the
work of God's grace. It is wrong to imagine that God gives
us so much help and then sits back to see whether or not
we will respond. Those whom he has chosen he saves effi-
caciously, infallibly. See the double warning in the middle
of p. 305, followed by more on cooperation with grace.
Calvin does not like the term but allows it in Augustine's
sense. Note the concession in the first sentence on p. 306,
though the words "by our own power" go beyond the Latin
ultro. Calvin immediately adds that any responsiveness on
our part is brought about by the Holy Spirit.

[§12. First Corinthians 15:10 is wrongly interpreted to mean
that we share the credit with God's grace. §§13–14 are
a further appeal to Augustine. The last sentence of §14
summarizes the case.]

[2.4. How God Works in the Human Heart. Calvin considers the respective roles of God, Satan, and ourselves in human choices, especially those of the ungodly. Calvin sees "no inconsistency in assigning the same deed to God, Satan, and man" (§2). God works out his purposes through the choices made by Satan and by people. In §§6–8, Calvin asks what freedom humanity has in morally neutral matters. His view is summarized in the first paragraph of §7.]

2.5. Refutation of Objections. Footnote 13 is of interest.

§1. Objection 1 comes in the fourth sentence. It is because of the *fall* that sin is necessary, but it nonetheless remains voluntary, as shown in 2.3.5.

§2. Objection 2 is stated in the first sentence. Vices are worthy of punishment because they are *voluntary* (par. 2). God does reward our virtues, but they are his gifts in that he works them in us (in pars. 3 and 4, read the first and last sentences).

§3. Objection 3 is stated in the first sentence.

§§4–5. Objection 4 is stated in the first sentence of §4. The answer is simply that God's grace works by means of exhortations and so forth. This is stated most clearly in the last paragraph of §5.

§§6–7. Objection 5, stated in the second paragraph of §6, is that "ought" implies "can,"[1] command implies ability. God does not command the impossible. But God's law reflects his holy standards, not the capacity of *fallen* humanity. God commands nothing that is impossible for humanity *as created*, but sinners are no longer capable of obedience. Calvin argues forcefully and with justice from Paul and from Augustine.

[§§8–13 consider further the biblical commands, promises, and reproofs together with other passages.]

1. The claim that "ought" implies "can" is found in Pelagius and, ironically, a philosopher whose name was Kant!

§§14–15. If God does it all, can we call our good works *our* good works? In some sense, yes. Especially notice the Augustine quotations in the fifth paragraph of §14 and the second paragraph of §15. In the first paragraph of §15, Calvin approves Augustine's statement that grace restores rather than destroys the will.

[§§16–19 consider five biblical passages cited against Calvin's view. The last sentence of §18 says, "Man now needs a physician, not an advocate." The priority is not to argue that human nature is better than it is, but rather to turn to the cure for the disease. The last three sentences of §19 give a summary of Calvin's pessimistic view of fallen humanity as taught in 2.1–5.]

10

The Place of the Law
(2.6.1, 4; 2.7.1–8, 10–15)

Introduction

Having described the dire condition of fallen humanity, Calvin argues that salvation is found in Christ alone (chap. 6). Law (in the Old Testament) was not given as an end in itself. It has three functions: to show us our need of Christ, to restrain the ungodly, and to guide believers (chap. 7).

Questions

What is the role of the law for the unbeliever? For the believer?

2.6. Salvation in Christ Alone. Footnotes 8 and 11 are of interest.

    §1. We need Christ because our natural knowledge of God does not suffice. Any "knowledge" of God is useless unless we come to know him as our *Father*. This is possible only through Christ. Therefore non-Christian religion and worship is false (par. 4).

[In §§2–3, Calvin offers Old Testament support for the claims of §1, showing that "the hope of all the godly has ever reposed in Christ alone" (§3).]

§4. There is no true faith in God and knowledge of God without faith in Christ and knowledge of Christ. See the last two sentences of paragraph 1. Line 4 of p. 347 should begin, "we cannot know him in a saving way." Toward the end of paragraph 2, Calvin again puts stress on knowing God as Father. Note also the last sentence on p. 347. It is of no value to recognize God's sovereignty (often mistakenly seen as the central point for Calvin) without knowing him as Father. This is applied to Muslims (Turks) on p. 348.

2.7. The Purpose of the Law. Footnotes 1–3, 9, 10, 20, and 21 are of interest.

§1. In the third sentence, Calvin defines "law." His definition is wider than what many understand by law. Calvin has a low view of the Mosaic ceremonies apart from their didactic purpose. The second paragraph can be skimmed after the first three sentences.

§2. Less important; may be skimmed. Calvin continues to stress the uselessness of the law without Christ. His argument is summarized in the last sentence of the first paragraph and the third sentence of the second paragraph.

§3. The law promises eternal life to those who obey it (par. 1). *But* we cannot obey it and therefore face death instead (par. 2). In the third sentence of this paragraph, Calvin says that the law is above human capacity—meaning *fallen* human capacity, as he makes explicit in §7.

§4. The law is not there just to mock us. Believers (justified by faith) can through their imperfect works receive the blessings promised to those who perfectly obey the law.

This is the doctrine of double justification, expounded in 3.17.1–10.[1]

§5. The observance of the law is impossible for us. No one has ever loved God perfectly. All are plagued with concupiscence/lust (par. 1). The second paragraph is less important and may be omitted.

The First Use or Function of the Moral Law (§§6–9)

§6. The law reveals our sin and cures us of our pride.

§7. The law is a mirror in which we see our failings. Also, the law provokes sin. The fault lies not with the law but with *us*. The law commends God's grace.

§8. The purpose of the law in all this is to drive us not to despair but to Christ; read the last three sentences.

[In §9, Calvin turns to Augustine, whose *The Spirit and the Letter* is devoted to this theme.]

The Second Function of the Law (§§10–11)

§10. The first two sentences explain this. The law restrains the ungodly from sin but without making them better. This is necessary for society and is useful in training those not yet converted.

§11 expounds Galatians 3:24, relating it to the first and second functions of the law in paragraphs 2 and 3.

The Third and Principal Use of the Law (§§12–15)

§12. The third and *principal* use of the law is for believers. The law is written on our hearts, but we also need the written law for ethical instruction (par. 2) and for exhortation (par. 3). There is much of practical value here.

§13. The "ignorant persons" who think believers do not need the law are still around today. Calvin insists on the abiding

---

1. Calvin himself does not use the term "double justification," though it was used by some of his contemporaries and is regularly used today.

applicability of the law (par. 1)—but will the application always remain the same? Believers should view the law as the goal toward which they strive in this life rather than as a rigorous policeman (par. 2).

§14. Has the law been abrogated for believers? It cannot bind our consciences with a curse (par. 1; cf. §15), but the *teaching* of the moral law is permanent (par. 2).

§15. The teaching of the law abides, but the believer is freed from its condemnation. More on this is in 3.19.1–6.

[§§16–17 concern the ceremonial law, fulfilled in Christ. In 4.20.14–15, Calvin affirms the traditional division of the law of Moses into moral, ceremonial, and judicial laws.]

11

Exposition of the Moral Law
(2.8.1–6, 8, 28–34, 51–55)

Introduction

After further general teaching about the role of law, Calvin expounds the Ten Commandments one by one.

Question

How does the law in general, and the fourth commandment in particular, function in our Christian lives?

2.8. Exposition of the Moral Law. Footnotes 1, 5–6, 13, 37, 40, 41, and 44 are of interest. [The set reading for this portion is about eighteen pages. Some may wish to read what Calvin says about *each* of the Ten Commandments, and the notes below are a guide to this. In fact Calvin's comments on most of the commandments are quite brief, with space being devoted to other issues, such as the promises attached.]

§1. The law convicts us of sin, the "first use" of the law (par. 1). All people have God's law written on their hearts in the form of conscience (natural law). But this is inadequate, so we need the written law as well.

§2. We are unable to keep the law. Yet we are still guilty because it is *our* fault that we cannot obey—the mystery of original sin.

§3. The psychology of conversion: the law leads us to self-awareness and thus drives us to God's mercy.

§4. God reinforces his law with promises and threats, which relate both to this life and to the next. The threats reveal God's holy purity; the promises reveal his generosity.

§5. Obedience means obeying God's commandments, no less and no *more*. We must not add to God's commandments—a common fault then as now.

§6. Nothing short of obedience from the heart will suffice to keep God's law. See the last sentence.

[In §7; the claims of §6 are supported by the teaching of Jesus.]

§8. We need to see the wider applications of each command. Read the first sentence, the sentence spanning pp. 374–75, and the last two sentences.

[§9 spells out further the principle stated in the last sentence of §8. When God forbids something, he expects of us not just negative abstention but the positive virtue. "You shall not kill" enjoins not just abstention from killing but also positively seeking our neighbor's good. Calvin follows this principle in his exposition of each of the commandments. §10 offers a further defense of the claims of §8. Then §11 talks of the two tables of the law: (1) our duties of religion toward God, and (2) our duties of love toward our fellow humans. Calvin claims that the latter cannot survive without the former. §12 discusses the numbering of the Ten

Commandments. §§13–16 expound the first commandment. §§13–15 are on the introductory material (Exod. 20:1–2), and only §16 is on the command itself. §§17–21 expound the second commandment, with just §17 on the command itself and §§18–21 on Exodus 20:5–6. This is surprisingly brief given that this was such a controversial commandment at that time, with the Reformed applying it against having images in church, as practiced by both Roman Catholics and Lutherans. The reason for this brevity is that a whole chapter (1.11) has already been devoted to the theme. §§22–27 expound the third commandment. As with the previous commands, §22 offers a brief exposition of the command, and §§23–27 discuss the issue of oaths, which was controversial since Anabaptists refused to swear them.]

§§28–34 expound the fourth commandment, on keeping the Sabbath.

§28. In paragraph 1 this commandment is in a different category from the other nine. In paragraph 2, Calvin lists three aspects of it, which he will expound.

§29. The idea of spiritual rest held the *chief place* (first sentence). Read the last three sentences.

§§30–31. The number seven denotes perpetuity (par. 2 of §30). In §31 we have a simpler explanation, set out in the first sentence. In the final paragraph, we see that the ceremonial is superseded. See the last sentence of §31.

§32. The Sabbath is abrogated, but there remains the twofold need for a day to be set aside for public worship and for employees to rest. The last paragraph meets the objection that we ought to meet *daily*.

§33. The difference between the Christian use of Sunday and the Jewish observance of the Sabbath. Sunday is a practical arrangement, not a sacred ceremony.

§34. No legalistic bondage to the number seven (par. 1). Paragraph 2 is a useful summary of Calvin's position. In paragraph 3 he attacks the "trifles of the false prophets," as found in late-medieval Roman Catholicism, the view that the command is part of the moral law except for the particular day of the week, which is ceremonial and can be changed (from Saturday to Sunday). Ironically, this view of Sunday as the Christian Sabbath became popular among British Calvinists and is expressed in the 1646/47 Westminster Confession of Faith (21.7–8).

[§§35–50 expound the last six commandments. Two sections are devoted to each commandment, except for the fifth and seventh commandments. The fifth commandment has an extra two sections (§§37–38) on the promise and threat that accompany the commandment. Calvin also devotes four sections to expounding the seventh commandment and its implications for celibacy (§42) and modesty (§44) as well as fidelity in marriage (§43).]

§51. On the purpose of the law, notice the first two sentences. The two great commandments (par. 2). Therefore we cannot progress beyond the law (sent. 1 of par. 3).

§§52–53. Why Scripture sometimes mentions only the second table of the law. Especially see §52, paragraph 2, last three sentences. This is supported by the prophets (par. 3). §53 is less important. The first table has priority; our love for others is evidence of our love for God.

§54. The importance of loving one another. Read the last sentence of each paragraph.

§55. Our love should extend to *all* people, though in varying degrees. We should love them "in God, not in themselves." See the last sentence.

[§§56–57 attack the Roman Catholic distinction between precepts (commands obligatory for all) and counsels (commands that are optional extras). The latter included voluntary poverty and celibacy, but Calvin chooses to focus on those who had also put love of enemy in this category. §§58–59 denounce the Roman Catholic distinction between venial and mortal sins. Calvin argues that all sins are mortal (as in Rom. 6:23) but makes no mention of 1 John 5:16–17, which states that not all sin is mortal.]

12

Relation between the Old and New Testaments
(2.9.1–4; 2.10.1–5; 2.11.1, 4, 7, 9–11)

Introduction

Chapter 9 discusses the relation between law given in the Old Testament and gospel given in the New Testament; it was added in 1559, primarily in response to Servetus. The following two chapters unpack the similarities and dissimilarities between the Testaments. There is essentially one covenant for all believers, whether before or after Christ (chap. 10). There are differences in the administration of this covenant, of which Calvin enumerates five (chap. 11).

Question

What are the similarities and the differences between the Old Testament and the New Testament?

2.9. Christ Known under the Law, Clearly Revealed in the Gospel. Footnote 1 is of interest.

§1. Less important; to be skimmed. The Old Testament saints knew Christ in an indistinct, shadowed way; to us he has appeared in visible form.

§2. In the first part, Calvin defines the term "gospel." In the broad sense this includes the promises of God in the Old Testament; in the strict sense it means "the proclamation of the grace manifested in Christ."

§3. The importance of the already/not yet tension. Check the last two sentences.

§4. The Lutheran contrast between law and gospel, between the merit of works and the forgiveness of sins—such a contrast has a certain validity (par. 1). But the gospel fulfills the law rather than supplanting it. They are *not* different ways of salvation. Indeed, "where the whole law is concerned, the gospel differs from it only in clarity of manifestation" (par. 2). Calvin can talk like this because for him "law" is pentateuchal or Old Testament *religion* (cf. definition in 2.7.1). For Luther, "law" means God's *demands* (in line with his experience before his conversion), as opposed to his promises.

[In §5 Calvin shows where John the Baptist fits in.]

2.10. The Similarity of Old and New Testaments. Footnotes 1, 2, 4, and 9 are of interest.

§1. Since the beginning of the world, all believers have had the same law, doctrine, and salvation. Note the first three sentences especially. Calvin's opponents are "that wonderful rascal Servetus and certain madmen of the Anabaptist sect." To their number would need to be added many modern critical Old Testament scholars.

§2. The second and third sentences summarize Calvin's position: one covenant with differing modes of administration. In paragraph 2, Calvin states three points about the Old Testament that emphasize its unity with the New Testament.

§3. The first point: Old Testament belief in immortality. Most today would agree that Calvin overstates his case here. Observe how the references in §3 are all to the *New* Testament. But clearly there is *some* evidence of belief in a future life found in the Old Testament.

§4. The second and third points: the Old Testament was based on God's free mercy and on Christ as Mediator (sent. 1). The last sentence summarizes Calvin's position.

§5. Old Testament and New Testament sacraments are essentially the same. This is a distinctively Reformed position. It has important implications for infant baptism; see 4.14 and 4.16.

[§6 answers an objection to §5. §§7–10 argue that Old Testament believers looked to a life beyond this one. §§10–22 demonstrate this from a range of Old Testament figures, from Adam to the prophets. Battles lists the figures cited and shows how §§10–22 parallel Hebrews 11.[1] Calvin stresses that many of them did not prosper in *this* life but looked to a future hope. Calvin clearly did not believe that worldly prosperity is a mark of election. §23 offers summary and conclusion. "The Old Testament . . . contained a promise of spiritual and eternal life."]

2.11. The Differences between the Old and New Testaments.
Footnote 2 is of interest. Battles has a chart summarizing the similarities and differences between the Old Testament and the New.[2]

§1. Five differences are to be identified in this chapter. All relate to the administration of the covenant rather than its substance (pars. 1 and 2). The first difference: In the Old Testament our heavenly heritage is displayed under earthly benefits; not so in the New Testament. The earthly benefits were a mirror (again) in which they saw their heavenly inheritance (last sentence).

1. Battles, *Analysis of the Institutes*, 142.
2. Ibid., 147.

[§2. Old Testament believers looked beyond this life. §3. But earthly benefits were used to foreshadow spiritual benefits.]

§4. The second difference: The Old Testament shows an image where the New Testament reveals the substance. This is explained from Hebrews.

[§5. The time under the law can be compared to childhood. §6. Even the prophets were lacking in knowledge because Christ had not yet come.]

§7. The third difference: As spelled out in Jeremiah 31:31–34 and 2 Corinthians 3:6–11, the new covenant is written on our hearts, not on tablets of stone.

[§8. The contrast is between letter and Spirit; between condemnation and death, on one hand, and righteousness and life on the other; between things temporary and ceremonial, on one hand, and abiding substance on the other.]

§§9–10. The fourth difference: The old covenant enslaves while the new liberates (§9). Yet the promises of the gospel *predate* the law. The elect in Old Testament times belonged to the new covenant because their faith was in Christ/God's promise (§10).

§11. The fifth difference: One nation versus all people.

[§12. The New Testament brings the calling of the Gentiles. §13. Some accuse God of fickleness, but he was wisely adapting to changing times. §14. God made these changes not for his own pleasure but to bring about our salvation.]

13

The Person of Jesus Christ
(2.12.1–3; 2.13.1, 4; 2.14.1–4)

Introduction

Because of human sin, there needed to be a Mediator who was both God and human, though ultimately this happened only because God willed it (chap. 12). Having argued for the deity of Christ in 1.13, Calvin now argues for his true humanity (chap. 13). He then reaffirms the Chalcedonian doctrine that Christ is one person in two natures (chap. 14).

Question

How does Calvin portray the person of Christ?

2.12. The Need for the Incarnation

§1. It was necessary for us that our Mediator be both God and human. But Christ became man because God willed it, not because of an *absolute* necessity. Here Calvin differs from Anselm. He follows in the tradition of Duns Scotus, who stressed the primacy of God's will rather than his reason. Things are the way they are because God *willed* it. We will meet this idea again later in Calvin. On p. 465, Calvin introduces the rather gloomy idea that humanity needed a mediator even before the fall. At the end there is a stress on Christ's true humanity.

§2. Christ came to save us. In the third and fifth sentences, Calvin echoes the patristic idea of Christ becoming what we are in order to make us what he is (for which see also 4.17.2, 4). He has come to make us his brothers and sisters (par. 1). It was therefore necessary for him to be both divine and human (par. 2).

§3. In the first paragraph, Calvin summarizes the argument of Anselm's *Why God Became Man*, including the idea that Christ's death was a *satisfaction* offered to God. He also introduces the idea of Christ paying our penalty, less prominent in Anselm. This recurs in the final sentence of the section.

[§§4–7 refute the idea that the Son would have become incarnate even if Adam had not fallen. This idea originated with Duns Scotus, but Calvin is attacking two of his own contemporaries.]

2.13. Christ's True Humanity. Footnote 2 is of interest.

§1. Scripture proves Christ's true humanity. Calvin presents a strong case, but in common with his contemporaries he understood "Son of Man" to mean "true man."

[§2 refutes Marcion and Mani. §3 affirms that Mary was Christ's true mother, against the idea of Menno Simons that she was only his "host mother."]

§4. Christ is truly human, but without sin because he was conceived by the Holy Spirit. In the last two sentences Calvin affirms that the incarnate Word was not confined to his human body. As God, he continued to fill the whole universe. Calvin was here following the early fathers, including Cyril, Leo, and Chalcedon. The Lutherans objected to this point and called it the "Extra-Calvinisticum" because of the teaching that the Word existed outside of (Latin, *extra*) the body.

2.14. One Person in Two Natures. Footnotes 1, 3, and 4 are of interest.

§1. The Word became flesh, but there is no confusion or mingling of the natures (against Eutyches). (The second sentence is more accurately translated as by Allen: "Choosing from the womb of the virgin a temple for his residence"— i.e., his body, which he received from her.) In Christ, divinity and humanity are united but remain distinct. Calvin's emphasis is similar to that of Pope Leo I in his *Tome*, which was approved at the Council of Chalcedon (AD 451). He is partly opposing the Lutherans (par. 1). The union of two natures in Christ is compared to the union of body and soul in humanity, a comparison that often occurs in the fathers. The last sentence on p. 482 echoes the controversial last sentence of the *Formula of Reunion*, the document accepted by Cyril of Alexandria in AD 433 to restore peace after the Council of Ephesus (AD 431). In the last two sentences, Calvin refers to the "communicating of properties." This is the practice of making statements about the deity of Christ that strictly refer to his humanity and vice versa, such as "God died for us" or "the universe was created through Jesus." Calvin gives some examples in §2.

§2. Scripture shows that Christ is both God (par. 1) and human (par. 2) and speaks of the "communicating of properties" (par. 3). On the last point, see the final sentence.

§3. Scripture also teaches the unity of Christ, in John (par. 1) and Paul (par. 2). The third paragraph, on the significance of the term "Lord," can be omitted.

§4. Paragraph 1: the scriptural teaching on these points is clear when they are rightly interpreted. Read the sentence leading to footnote 8. This is the role that Calvin saw for his *Institutes* (p. 6). Paragraph 2: Christ's two natures are united, not mingled (against Eutyches) and not divided (against Nestorius). Calvin explicitly approves the councils of Ephesus and Chalcedon, which condemned these two heretics. Notice the last sentence.

[§§5–8 oppose the errors of Servetus.]

14

The Redemptive Work
of Jesus Christ
(2.15.1, 3–4, 6; 2.16.1–7,
10–11, 13–19)

Introduction

Christ was sent by God to be prophet, king, and priest (chap. 15). He saved us by his whole life of obedience and especially by bearing our sins on the cross (chap. 16). Christ merited God's grace and salvation for us (chap. 17).

Questions

What are the three offices of Christ (2.15)? How has he won our salvation (2.16)?

2.15. Christ as Prophet, King, and Priest. Footnotes 2, 3, 9–11, and 15 are of interest.

§1. In the second paragraph Calvin introduces the three offices of Christ, an idea that goes back to Eusebius of Caesarea and was taught by Bucer. In the final paragraph he begins his exposition of Christ as prophet, to which the Old Testament bears witness.

[**§2.** More on Christ as prophet. Christ receives this gift for his church as well as for himself (Joel 2:28), but we need no more prophecies that go beyond the simple gospel of Jesus Christ (1 Cor. 2:2).]

§§3–4. As king, Christ is the eternal protector and defender of the church (§3, par. 1), and so eternal preservation of the church is guaranteed (par. 2). But this does *not* mean that the church will have an easy time. The Christian hope is for the age to come (par. 3, developed in 3.9). §4 develops the ideas of earthly adversity and heavenly hope.

[**§5** develops further aspects of Christ's kingly role.]

§6. Christ as priest, also the theme of 2.16. The first four sentences sum it up. In the second paragraph we see Christ as both priest and sacrifice. Also, he makes us priests with him—but there is no place for "the sacrifice of the Mass" (attacked in 4.18).

2.16. Christ's Work of Redemption. Footnotes 1, 23, 25, 34, and 39 are of interest.

§1. Salvation is found only in Christ (par. 1). As we look within, we see our sin, our guilt, God's wrath toward us, and therefore our need for an adequate salvation.

§§2–4. We are told that before the cross we were God's enemies and under his wrath. These things are said to show us how serious our plight is apart from Christ. In fact, though, it was because God already loved us that he gave his Son for us. This argument is stated in the first two paragraphs of §2 and summarized in the last. §§3–4 pursue this further, considering how, before the cross, God both loved and hated us. Read the last two sentences of §3 and the last three of §4.

§5. Christ saved us by his whole life of obedience rather than by the cross alone (par. 1), but it was especially by the cross (par. 2). It had to be a *judicial* death, not any old death (par. 3). He was innocent (in himself) but guilty (because of us).

§6. Christ bore our punishment in his place, an important section. Neither here nor anywhere else does Calvin speak of God punishing Christ. He holds to Christ's role in bearing the consequences of our sin without imperiling the unity of the Father and the Son.

§7. "By dying, he ensured that we would not die" (par. 1). Through his death, our old self is put to death (par. 2). Summary is in paragraph 3.

[§§8–9. The "descent into hell" (Apostles' Creed). The importance of this clause (§8) and some wrong interpretations of it in Calvin's time (§8) and earlier (§9).]

§§10–11. Calvin's interpretation of the clause. Christ descended into hell in that *on the cross* he "suffered the death that God in his wrath had inflicted upon the wicked" (§10). Christ felt himself to be forsaken by God and experienced the effects of God's wrath, but the Father was not actually hostile toward him (§11). Calvin holds the nuanced position that Christ's death appeased God's wrath (§10) but that the Father was never actually angry toward his beloved Son (§11). Christ "experienced all the signs of a wrathful and avenging God" (§11).

[§12 answers objections to Calvin's interpretation of the clause.]

§13. Our salvation requires the resurrection as well as the cross. See the summary in lines 7–12 of p. 521. Three benefits of the resurrection: Christ is our Mediator, who gives us a new life of righteousness now, and guarantees our future resurrection.

§14. The importance of the ascension for our salvation, shown from Scripture.

§15. The scriptural significance of Christ being seated at the right hand of the Father.

§16. The three paragraphs set out three benefits of §§14–15 for us today.

§§17–18. Christ's return to judge humanity. Summary of scriptural teaching (§17). Believers have the assurance that this judge is none other than their Savior (§18, par. 1). The Apostles' Creed has been followed as a useful scriptural summary of the basic essentials of Christ's work for us, regardless of its origin and authorship (§18, par. 2).

§19. Return to the theme of §1: salvation is in Christ alone.

[2.17. Christ Has Merited God's Grace and Salvation. This chapter responds to questions raised especially by Laelius Socinus (n. 1), who held that salvation is by God's mercy alone, without any regard to Christ's merit. Calvin agreed that salvation is totally because of God's mercy, but he also argues that "by his obedience . . . Christ truly acquired and merited grace for us with his Father" (§3).]

BOOK 3

The Way in Which We
Receive the Grace of Christ

What Benefits Come to Us from It,
and What Effects Follow

Book 2 has explained what Christ has achieved for our benefit;
book 3 shows how we can individually appropriate this. The
work of Christ benefits us only when we are united with him,
and this is effected by the Holy Spirit through faith (chap. 1).
After a long and important chapter on faith itself (chap. 2),
Calvin devotes eight chapters each to the two benefits that we
enjoy in Christ: justification and sanctification. To emphasize
that there is no justification without sanctification, Calvin expounds the latter first. He explains the meaning of regeneration
and repentance (chap. 3), contrasting the latter with the Roman
Catholic doctrines of confession and satisfaction (chap. 4)
and indulgences and purgatory (chap. 5). Then he devotes five

chapters to the theme of the Christian life (chaps. 6–10). The exposition of justification by faith includes discussion of the role of works and the basis for reward (chaps. 11–18). After the lengthy discussion of sanctification and justification come chapters on Christian freedom (chap. 19) and on prayer (chap. 20). These are followed by a sustained discussion of election and reprobation (chaps. 21–24). Book 3 ends with a chapter on the final resurrection (chap. 25).

15

Saving Faith
(3.1.1, 4; 3.2.6–7, 10–11, 14–19, 22–24, 36)

Introduction

The work of Christ, just described, benefits us only when the Holy Spirit unites us to him by faith (chap. 1). A long and important chapter defines and expounds the nature of saving faith (chap. 2).

Questions

What is faith? What is its object, and on what is it based?

3.1. The Inner Work of the Holy Spirit. Footnote 9 is of interest.

  §1. Notice the third sentence. Christ's work is "useless and of no value for us" until we are united to him. This work (described in book 2) is "for the salvation of the human race." Calvin appears to teach that Christ's work is for all, but the application of it is only for some.[1] This union comes through faith, which is the inner work of the Holy Spirit.

[§2. New Testament teaching on Christ's relationship to the Spirit. §3. Scriptural titles of the Holy Spirit, such as "spirit of adoption," "guarantee and seal" of our inheritance.]

§4. Faith is the principal work of the Holy Spirit, the inner teacher. Especially see the sentences that follow the reference to Ephesians 1:13 and include 2 Corinthians 3:6.

3.2. Definition and Nature of Faith. Footnotes 25 and 36 are of interest.

[§1. Faith is more than just mental assent to doctrine. Faith is in Christ specifically, not just in God in general. §§2–5 reject the Roman Catholic idea of "implicit faith," the idea that it is sufficient merely to give blanket assent to whatever the church teaches. The essence of faith is "the knowledge of God and Christ" (§3).]

§6. Faith is *knowledge* of Christ (first sentence). This faith is based upon *God's Word*. Faith is more than just a knowledge that God exists. It is a knowledge of his *will toward us*, by which we know that he is our Father who loves us.

§7. Faith rests upon God's Word, in particular the *promises* of grace and mercy. In other words, it rests upon Christ, the sole pledge of God's love. The final sentence, the definition of faith, is the center of the whole chapter. It is expounded in §§14–37.

[§§8–9 attack the Roman Catholic distinction between "unformed faith" (mere intellectual assent) and "formed faith" (faith with love). Calvin is reluctant to count the former as "faith." See the note on 3.14.20, below, which reinforces

---

1. There has been considerable controversy about Calvin's relation to the later idea of limited atonement. He does not address the question directly, but the thrust of his teaching points to universal rather than limited atonement.

the point that only faith that works through love is real faith.]

§10. What of the "temporary faith" of reprobates such as Simon Magus, who "believe" for a time? Paragraph 2 explains this. Such folk are sincerely self-deceived. They have a mental assent to the truth, an assent that does not penetrate to the heart.

§11. The reprobates have a "faith" similar to the true faith of the elect, and they think themselves elect (par. 1). But they lack full assurance (par. 2). There is a lower and imperfect work of the Spirit in such folk, but they have no real grasp of God's grace and the forgiveness of sins (par. 3).

[§12. More on the similarities and differences between true and temporary faith. §13. How is the term "faith" used in Scripture? We need to return to the definition of saving faith.]

§§14–19 take up the definition of faith from the end of §7.

§14. Faith as *knowledge*, yet faith transcends ordinary knowledge (sents. 3 and 4). See the last sentence.

§§15–16. Faith as certainty. The second paragraph is important. Faith is not simply believing in God's mercy *in general*. It is a belief that God is merciful to *me*. This point is further developed in §16. Notice the first sentence. On p. 562 Calvin holds that true faith is assurance of *my* salvation. But does this mean that anyone with doubts has no true faith? No.

§§17–18. Faith is constantly in conflict with doubt. *Faith* involves total conviction, but *we* have to struggle against unbelief. The first paragraph of §17 is important; the rest of §17 gives scriptural illustrations and may be skimmed. §18 talks of this inner conflict.

§19 sums up the discussion.

[§§20–21 continue the themes of faith versus doubt and of the weakness of our faith. Ultimately, faith will be victorious.]

§§22–24. The relation between faith and fear. Faith excludes the servile fear of those who are not God's children. It does not exclude the reverent fear appropriate to God's children. Confidence before God does not mean presumption or complacency. But with confidence we *are* to look forward to salvation on the basis of Christ, not on the basis of what is in us.

[§§25–27. More on faith and fear. §28. Faith relates to eternal life. §§29–32. Faith rests on God's *promises* in particular. §§33–35. It is the Holy Spirit who gives us faith.]

§36. Faith is not just a matter of the brain. It needs to take root in the *heart*, and this is through the work of the Holy Spirit, who seals God's promises upon our hearts. This also explains Calvin's style in the *Institutes*. He writes not just to inform the mind but also to move the will.

[§37. Faith and doubt. §§38–40. Faith is certainty of present *and* final salvation. §§41–43. Hope is the expectation of what faith believes to have been promised by God.]

16

Regeneration and Repentance
(3.3.1–12, 14, 19–20)

Introduction

Faith unites us to Christ (chaps. 1–2). *In Christ* we enjoy two
benefits: justification and sanctification. These are distinct but
cannot be separated. To make this point, Calvin discusses sanctification first (chaps. 3–10), then justification (chaps. 11–19).
He begins the former with an account of repentance, which for
him is a lifelong process roughly equivalent to sanctification
(chap. 3). After expounding the biblical doctrine of repentance,
he then attacks false views of it that have developed in Roman
Catholic theology and practice: confession to priests and the
need to offer "satisfaction" to God (chap. 4), and indulgences
and purgatory (chap. 5).

Questions

What is repentance? How does it relate to faith and to forgiveness?

3.3. Regeneration by Faith: Repentance. Footnotes 1–3, 9, 11, 14, 17, 19, and 30 are of interest.

§§1–2. The sum of the gospel is repentance and forgiveness (Luke 24:47; Acts 5:31)—in other words, sanctification and justification. These are distinct, but cannot be separated. Moreover, though there is no time lag between them, the order is faith leading to repentance, not vice versa.[1] (In lines 5–6 of p. 593, "constantly" should be "immediately.") We do not begin to obey God from the heart until we have been put right with him and see him as our Father. Obedience is the fruit of forgiveness, not vice versa.

§3. Repentance can be divided into mortification and vivification, which Calvin defines. We die to ourselves so that we can begin to live to God.

§4. Calvin offers definitions of legal and evangelical repentance. The legal kind is the sort of regret/remorse felt by the ungodly. It comes from a fear of God without any confidence in his forgiveness: fear without faith. The evangelical kind is the repentance of the believer, who fears/respects God but for whom this fear leads not to despair but to trust in his mercy.

§5. Repentance and faith are distinct but cannot be separated (par. 1). Paragraph 2 concludes with the definition of repentance, which is expounded in §§6–9. Paragraph 3 is less important and may be omitted.

§6. Repentance involves an inward change, a common biblical theme.

§7. Repentance arises from a fear of God. This means a hatred not just of *punishment* but also of *sin* itself.

§8. Repentance consists of mortification and vivification, as in §3.

---

1. But Calvin also acknowledges elsewhere that there is a "beginning of repentance," which is a "preparation for faith" (commentary on Acts 20:21 in *Calvin's Commentaries: The Acts of the Apostles 14–28*, trans. J. Fraser [Edinburgh: Saint Andrew Press, 1966], 176–77).

§9. Both of these come from participation in Christ. Calvin equates repentance with regeneration, both being a lifelong process of sanctification. While they may have a beginning, neither is seen as a once-for-all act. It is a lifelong process.

§10. Because regeneration is a lifelong process, perfection does not come at once. In the Christian, there is a "smoldering cinder of evil," the source of sinful desires. These desires Calvin calls sin, in line with the other Reformers but contrary to the Catholic tradition.

§11. When we become Christians, sin no longer *reigns* over us, but it *remains* in us. Thus conversion is the *beginning* rather than the end of our struggle against sin. God does not hold us guilty for our sinful desires—not because they do not warrant it, but because we are forgiven in Christ. The second paragraph (esp. sentence 3) defends this.

§12. Our human desires are sinful, not because God made them that way, but because of the fall. In fallen humanity they have become *inordinate*. Sexual desire becomes lust, the need for food becomes gluttony, and so forth. Advertising agencies know all about this and exploit it. This is the way we are now but not the way God created us.

[§13 calls on Augustine as a witness for Calvin's view.]

§14. In paragraph 1, Calvin describes an extreme form of perfectionism, which was around then and has cropped up since then in various more "enthusiastic" groups. In the second paragraph, Calvin refutes this teaching. In the last paragraph, he offers his alternative to perfectionism: slow but steady progress toward perfection, involving a daily struggle against sin, which is less glamorous but more biblical and realistic.

[§15. Exposition of 2 Corinthians 7:11. Read the quotation from Bernard in the last eight lines: we need to think on the Lord's goodness as well as on our own sinfulness. §16. The need for *inward* repentance. §§17–18. The outward aspects of repentance.]

103

§§19–20. The whole gospel is contained in the words "repentance" and "forgiveness of sins," which equal sanctification and justification, both of which are received by faith. (Calvin defines "the Kingdom of God" early in §19.) There is no forgiveness *without* repentance, but repentance is neither the *basis* of forgiveness nor a *prior* condition for it.

[§§21–25 discuss the vexed issue of the sin against the Holy Spirit, which Calvin sees as a willful rejection of the gospel by those who know that it is true, an "apostasy of the whole man." God never turns away those who repent, but such people are incapable of repentance.]

[3.4. Confession and Satisfaction. §§1–8, 15–25. An attack on the Roman Catholic doctrine and practice of penance. §§9–13. Confession is important, and this may be secretly to God or publicly (as in regular worship) or privately to one another or to a pastor. Those who have no assurance of forgiveness are free to confess privately to the pastor, who exercises the authority given in Matthew 16:19; 18:18; John 20:23 (§12). §14. The church has the authority to declare sins forgiven, but only in accordance with the gospel. §§26–27. Christ has made full satisfaction for our sins, so the Roman Catholic doctrine that we need to offer God satisfaction for sins committed after baptism is mistaken. §§28–36. Calvin rejects the Roman Catholic distinctions between mortal and venial sin (§28), between guilt and penalty (§§29–30), and between judgment/punishment of vengeance and of chastisement (§§31–36).]

[3.5. Indulgences and Purgatory. The Roman Catholic Church teaches that the church can dispense indulgences, which convey the merits of Christ and the saints, and that these indulgences can serve as a satisfaction for our sins. This teaching is contrary to Scripture (§§1–5). The biblical passages cited in support of the doctrine of purgatory do not in fact prove it (§§6–9). The early fathers were not without fault here but do not support the modern Roman doctrine (§10).]

17

The Christian Life: Self-Denial
(3.6; 3.7.1–2, 4–10)

Introduction

Calvin's concern to make the *Institutes* useful and practical is seen in the five chapters devoted to the Christian life. He considered these to be of such great importance that in 1550 he had them printed as a booklet on their own. He begins with general principles about the Christian life (chap. 6) and moves on to the specific commands of Matthew 16:24, starting with the need for self-denial (chap. 7).

Questions

What is the essence of the Christian life? How should self-denial affect our way of life?

3.6. The Essence of the Christian Life

§1. Calvin aims to give general principles rather than go into details (par. 3). He again refers to his love of brevity.

Scripture is not always "methodical" or systematic, but we can legitimately draw its scattered teaching together (par. 4).

§2. We need a love for righteousness *and* a rule to keep that zeal from being misdirected (par. 1). Above all, we need to share in God's holiness (par. 2). The last sentence states this forcefully. Also read the first two sentences of p. 686.

§3. The scriptural pattern differs from that of the philosophers: it is Christ himself. Calvin takes up the medieval theme of the imitation of Christ. Thus 3.6–10 are especially in the mold of the late-medieval *devotio moderna* (modern devotion), of which the best-known expression is Thomas à Kempis's *The Imitation of Christ*.

§4. A warning against nominal Christianity. Christian doctrine (including the *Institutes*) needs to penetrate to the heart, change us, and lead to practical daily living.

§5. An important section. Calvin's standards are high, but he is not a perfectionist (par. 1). It is wrong to lower our sights and to come to terms with sin (par. 2). Our expectation is not imminent perfection but slow, steady, daily progress, as is beautifully expressed in paragraph 3.

3.7. Self-Denial. Footnotes 1, 7, 8, and 10–12 are of interest.

§1. We are not our own, but we are God's. Check the last sentence of paragraph 4.

§2. Saying no to ourselves is the only way to progress in the Christian life. The last two sentences sum it up well.

[In §3 Calvin expounds Titus 2:11–14. Ungodliness and worldly desires are to be avoided. Soberness, righteousness, and godliness are our aims.]

§4. Self-denial is the way to get on well with others. This is because we are all plagued with pride and conceit, which cause strife with others. See the last sentence.

§5. Our money and our possessions are given to us to be used for others (esp. end of par. 1). The Christian pattern is stewardship—not merely our giving 10 percent of our money, but using it *all* as stewards of God's gifts, which have been given to us for the common good.

§6. How should we view our needy fellow humans? We are to love them not because of their merit (which most of them do not have) but because we see God's image in them. The last sentence sums this up.

§7. Christian giving is not "cold charity." We must truly empathize, as taught in the last sentence of paragraph 1. Such an attitude spells an end to a legalism imagining that a tithe of 10 percent or any other percentage is the measure of Christian giving. Calvin's standards are much higher, as is clearly stated in the last sentence.

§8. We should submit to God's will and not seek prosperity in any way contrary to that will. It is clear that Calvin was anything but an uncritical supporter of consumerism and that he should not be seen as the father of prosperous bourgeois Christianity.

§9. In the light of God's providence, we should trust him alone. We should not strive for wealth or honors but follow the course that he has set for us.

§10. If we are denying ourselves, and if we trust God's providence, we will be able to bear whatever adversity he might send. The last sentence of paragraph 1 sums this up. We are in the hands not of blind fortune but of God's providence, as restated in the last sentence.

18

The Christian Life:
Bearing Our Cross
and Attitude toward This Life
(3.8.1–7; 3.9; 3.10.1–5)

Introduction

The exposition of Matthew 16:24 continues with a chapter on bearing the cross, which is an aspect of self-denial (chap. 8). It is only as we meditate on the life to come that we can have the right attitude toward this present life (chap. 9). When we have grasped that, we can learn how to use the things of this world correctly (chap. 10).

Questions

Why do we need to bear our cross (3.8)? How should we regard this life and the next (3.9–10)?

3.8. Bearing the Cross. Footnote 5 is of interest.

§1. If *Christ* had to bear his cross, why should we be exempt? In bearing our cross, we follow his example, share in his sufferings, and thus progress toward salvation. Furthermore, the cross has many benefits in our life, as explained in §§2–7.

§2. It humbles our pride by showing us our incapacity and weakness. It curbs our complacency and self-sufficiency.

§3. It teaches us to put our confidence not in the flesh but in God. He has helped us in the past and will do so again.

§4. The cross tests our patience and teaches us obedience.

§5. It is the medicine that we need to curb the wantonness of the flesh. "Fattened and made flabby, we kick against him who has fed and nourished us." We each receive different doses, but no child of God is exempt from the medicine.

§6. Above all, in our tribulations we should see the fatherly hand of God, who is working for our salvation. We must be sure to respond rightly to his chastisement (p. 707).

§7. It is a great honor to suffer for righteousness's sake.

[**§§8–11.** We are to rejoice in our suffering, but this does not mean that we do not truly suffer. We rejoice *in* suffering, not *instead of* suffering. The Christian ideal is not Stoic impassibility, immunity from feelings or sorrow, but patience and cheerfulness *in* pain and sorrow. Christians can bear tribulations patiently because we know that our Father sends them *for our good*. (This is a much-needed emphasis today, when there is a tendency to expect God's power to remove our weakness rather than work through it.)]

3.9. Meditation on the Future Life

§1. We commonly live as if only this life matters. The misfortunes of life serve to keep us from such an attitude. Read the last two sentences.

§2. The first sentence poses a stark choice. The last sentence of paragraph 1 points to the dangers of our comfortable, affluent society. We acknowledge our mortality in theory, but in practice we live most of the time as if we were immortal. Most of us have too much love for this life (par. 2).

§3. While this life is to be despised *relative to* the life to come, in itself it contains much that is good, as long as our sights are set beyond it.

§4. Compared with the life to come, our earthly life is to be despised. We are exiles looking for a future homeland. The body is a prison from which we will be released.

§5. Christians should not fear death but see it as our recall from exile. It is monstrous that many Christians are terrified of death (first sentence). Also notice the last sentence of paragraph 1. Calvin does not forget Christ's return and the resurrection, but he more often refers to *death* as the point at which we attain our goal. In the New Testament, the emphasis is stronger on Christ's return as the point where full salvation is received.

§6. Our "sole comfort" is the prospect of the life to come. See the last sentence.

3.10. **How to Use the Things of This World.** Footnote 4 is of interest.

§1. We should use the things of this world insofar as they *help* our Christian discipleship (par. 1). We need to keep the balance between legalistic asceticism and unrestrained self-indulgence (pars. 2 and 3). Scripture does not bind our consciences with legalistic rules in this area, but it does set out general principles that we must follow.

§2. The chief principle is found in sentence 1. God has given us things for our enjoyment as well as for our necessity (last sentence).

§3. But this does not justify excessive self-indulgence. We are to enjoy food and wine without gluttony or drunkenness. We are to use God's gifts, not abuse them.

§4. Two more rules: use temporal gifts without being enslaved to them, and be willing to lose them. We are to live frugally and without ostentation.

§5. The second and third principles are contentment (par. 1) and stewardship (par. 2).

[§6. We are each to keep to the vocation to which God has called us, which is how to please God.]

19

Justification by Faith
(3.11.1–2, 7, 16–17, 21, 23;
3.12.1–2, 4–8; 3.13.3; 3.14.1–4)

Introduction

Having expounded sanctification (chaps. 3–10), Calvin now
turns to the second benefit of union with Christ: justification.
He begins by defining it as the forgiveness of sins and imputa-
tion of Christ's righteousness (chap. 11). A sober analysis of
our own righteousness shows that our only hope lies in God's
mercy (chap. 12). Justification by faith gives glory to God and
brings us peace of conscience (chap. 13). Even the virtues of the
unregenerate have no value for righteousness (chap. 14).

Questions

What is justification? Why must it be by faith alone?

3.11. Justification by Faith Defined

§1. Christ gives us both justification and sanctification. The latter has been considered first (3.3–10) to make clear that there is no faith without good works. Calvin now turns to justification, which is "the main hinge on which religion turns." Three lines up from the bottom of the text on p. 725, "the second of these gifts" should be "the second grace."

§2. The definition of justification: see the second sentence and the last three.

[§§3–4 present scriptural support for the definition of §2. §§5–12 combat the views of Osiander, a contemporary Lutheran theologian, whose niece married Thomas Cranmer. Osiander failed to distinguish clearly between justification and sanctification. These two are indeed inseparable but are also distinct from one another, like the heat and light of the sun (§6). Calvin famously (and only this once) calls our union with Christ a "mystical union" (§10; see n. 20).[1]]

§7. It is *Christ* who justifies. Faith merely unites us to him and receives his righteousness.

[§13. Scripture starkly contrasts faith righteousness and works righteousness. §§14–15. The medieval theologians went sadly astray here.]

§16. The scriptural way of salvation: trust in God's mercy/ Christ's righteousness *alone*. Even when as Christians we do "good works," our trust is not in these.

§17. Faith embraces a free and unconditional righteousness promised in the gospel. The law demands good works as a condition for righteousness. Christians have love but are not justified by it, for the reason given in the last sentence.

[§§18–20. Justification is by faith *alone* and apart from the merit of works. "No other faith justifies 'but faith working through love' [Gal. 5.6]"—but it is the faith that justifies (by uniting us to Christ), not the love (§20).]

---

1. On this theme, see D. E. Tamburello, *Union with Christ: John Calvin and the Mysticism of St. Bernard* (Louisville: Westminster John Knox, 1994).

§21. Calvin returns to the definition of §2 and defends it. He argues that justification is the forgiveness of sins, free acceptance by God.

[§22 provides scriptural support.]

§23. Justification is also the reckoning or imputing to us of Christ's righteousness; it is only *in him*, as partakers in him, that we are righteous.

3.12. God's Judgments Show Our Need of Free Justification. Footnote 2 is of interest.

§§1–2. Our human righteousness may look good until we test it by God's standards, which are nothing less than perfection. Read the second sentence of §1 and the sixth ("Yet surely . . . any corruption ."). If you agree with these, Calvin's conclusion follows. It is only when we know God and his purity that we truly know ourselves as sinners (see 1.1.2–3).

[§3. Calvin appeals to Augustine and to Bernard of Clairvaux for support.]

§§4–5. We need a true assessment of our works, based on the need for purity of *heart*, not just outward performance.

§§6–7. We need a genuine humility—not a forced pretense of modesty but a sober and realistic recognition of what we actually are.

§8. Arrogance and complacency are the two obstacles to people's coming to Christ. God's grace is received when we abandon all self-confidence and cast ourselves on him.

3.13. Justification by Faith Gives Glory to God and Peace of Conscience to Us

[§§1–2. The doctrine of justification by faith gives glory to God.]

§3. We can have peace of mind if we are justified by faith alone, not if our justification depends (even in part) on our merit, works, or observance of the law.

[§4. God's promises are nullified if we rely on our own righteousness. §5. Our hope is to be entirely in the promise of God's grace. See the last sentence: "For, as regards justification, faith is something merely passive, bringing nothing of ours to the recovering of God's favor but receiving from Christ that which we lack."]

3.14. Beginning and Continuation of Justification

The Virtues of Pagans (§§1–4; see also 2.3.1–4)

§1. In the first paragraph, Calvin lists four types of people. The first three lines of the second paragraph contain a forthright statement about unregenerate humanity. Do you agree? If not, read on and look for the weakness in Calvin's argument.

§2. Calvin acknowledges that there is a difference between virtue and vice among non-Christians and sees the virtue as a gift of God.

§§3–4. But such pagan virtues are of no value for righteousness before God. They deserve punishment. Why? Because the motivation of the heart is wrong. Here there is what one might call a soft and a hard position. The hard position, which Calvin adopts, is that *every* deed of the ungodly is sinful. The soft position, which Calvin rejects, would be that the ungodly may perform worthy deeds but that they cannot be justified by works because they also sin in many ways and deserve punishment. The soft position suffices to establish the doctrine of justification by faith, but Calvin argues for the harder position. Do you agree with him?

[§§5–6 develop this argument. §§7–8 extend the argument to cover nominal Christians and hypocrites, the second and third types mentioned at the beginning of §1.]

115

20

The Value of Our Good Works
(3.14.9–11, 18–19, 21;
3.16; 3.17.3, 8–10)

Introduction

Even the good works of Christians cannot justify us (chap. 14). God rewards our works, but they should not be seen as meritorious (chap. 15). Justification is not by works, but nor is it without works (chap. 16). As well as accepting us in Christ, God also accepts our good works in him (chap. 17). God rewards our works, but we should not imagine that they actually have any value (chap. 18).

Questions

Of what value are our good works (3.14)? What incentives are there to do good works (3.16–17)?

3.14. Beginning and Continuation of Justification (cont.). Calvin considers the good works of the genuine Christian, the fourth of the types mentioned in §1.

§9. Conversion brings a real change (par. 1). But even our best works, judged by the standards of God's holiness, are tainted. See the final sentence. Here again there are soft and hard positions. The soft position would be that as believers we still sin frequently. The hard position, which Calvin holds, is that even as believers our best works fall short of perfection. Do you agree with him?

§10. Even if we performed one perfect work, it would be tainted by our sin. The law demands unceasing obedience, not just occasional conformity.

§11. Paragraph 1 summarizes §§9–10. We are justified by faith not just at the beginning of the Christian life, but truly throughout.

[§§12–17 oppose Roman Catholic errors, especially the idea that we can perform "works of supererogation" by doing more than God requires of us and thus acquire merit (§§13–16). §17 sets out the four causes of salvation, following the philosophical division: the efficient, material, formal/instrumental, and final causes. These are summarized more briefly in §21.]

§18. Is there any place for works in assurance of salvation? If we *first* have confidence before God on the basis of his mercy, we can *then* receive encouragement from our good works, which are evidences of God's working in us. But works must never become the basis of our assurance before God.

§19. More on this theme. Because of their imperfections, our good works are not a sound basis for assurance. But to those who are justified by faith alone, they are an encouraging evidence of God's work in us.

[§20 contains more on this theme.]

§21. Calvin summarizes the fourfold cause of our salvation, stated more fully in §17. Salvation is by grace alone, but works *do* play a subsidiary role in salvation.

[3.15. No Boasting about Merit. This opposes Roman Catholic teaching on the merit of good works. Calvin would rather avoid the term "merit," but he agrees that our good works are not without value (§2), though elsewhere he repeatedly stresses that our works are worthless. Our good works are acceptable to God and he rewards them, not because they merit/deserve this, but because of his generosity (§3). We, "without reference to merit, still remarkably cheer and comfort the hearts of believers by our teaching, when we tell them that they please God in their works and are without doubt acceptable to him" (§7, par. 4). How and why God accepts these works is explained in 3.17.8–10 as "double justification." The tension between even our best works being tainted (3.14.9) and God's being pleased with our works is nicely expressed by the statement of George MacDonald: "God is easy to please but hard to satisfy."[1]]

3.16. Answer to Accusations That Justification by Faith Undermines Good Works. Footnotes 2 and 12 are of interest.

§1. Paragraph 1 states the Roman Catholic objections to which Calvin responds: Faith/justification cannot exist without good works, but we are justified by faith alone (par. 2). Faith unites us to Christ and therefore gives us justification *and* sanctification (par. 3). Justification and sanctification must be *distinguished*, but they cannot be *separated* because both are accomplished in Christ (par. 4). Justification is not by works, but nor is it without works.

§2. The first paragraph states the Roman Catholic objection. (Calvin will take up the issue of reward in 3.18.) Truly good works are performed *freely*, not just for a reward (par. 2). A stronger incentive is the fact that we are saved *for* good works (par. 3).

§§3–4. The strongest incentive to good works is the doctrine of salvation through God's mercy alone and the recogni-

1. As cited by C. S. Lewis, *Mere Christianity* (London: Collins, 1952), 168–69.

tion of what our salvation cost Christ. These truths lead us to shun sin. As Thomas Erskine put it, "Religion is grace and ethics is gratitude."[2]

3.17. The Promises of the Law and of the Gospel. Footnote 9 is of interest.

[§§1–2. The law contains promises, but works cannot obtain them.]

§3. Through the gospel we gain what the law promises. God accepts *us* in Christ. He then also accepts *our works* in him: double justification. This is because he overlooks the sinful defects in our works and accepts them as good.

[§4 cites the case of Cornelius (Acts 10). §5. Our good works are accepted *in Christ*. §§6–7. Biblical passages on the righteousness of works and how they are to be understood.]

§§8–10. More on double justification.

§8. This doctrine enables us to reconcile biblical teaching on justification by faith with that on God accepting our works. Paragraph 3 defines "justification," and paragraph 4 explains how God accepts our works.

§9 is less important.

§10. The fifth sentence defines "double justification." Calvin shows how this doctrine can be used to interpret biblical passages that speak of the value of our works.

[§§11–12 deal with the issue of Paul versus James. §§13–15 consider other passages that apparently contradict justification by faith, such as Romans 2:13.]

[3.18. Reward, Not Works Righteousness. How and why God rewards our good works. Calvin concedes that Scripture calls eternal life the reward of works, yet it is to be seen as sons' inheritance, not servants' wages (§§1–3). A significant statement comes at the beginning of §4, where

---

2. Thomas Erskine, *Letters of Thomas Erskine of Linlathen*, ed. William Hanna (Edinburgh: David Douglas, 1877), 16.

Calvin claims that Scripture's "whole end is to restrain our pride, to humble us, cast us down, and utterly crush us." Boosting our self-esteem was not Calvin's first priority. God rewards our works, but they "are pleasing to him only through pardon" (§5). God's generosity should not mislead us into thinking that our works have any worth (§§6–7). We are justified by faith, not because faith itself merits righteousness, but because it is the instrument by which we obtain Christ's righteousness (§8).]

21

The True Nature of Christian Freedom
(3.19.1–5, 7–15)

Introduction

Christian freedom means having a clear conscience, obeying God willingly and freely, and being free from legalistic regulations.

Question

What does Calvin understand by Christian freedom?

3.19. Christian Freedom. Footnotes 1, 9, 10, 13, and 16 are of interest.

    §1. This is an important topic related to justification (par. 1). We must steer a middle course between the extremes of license and legalism (par. 2).

The First Part of Christian Freedom (§§2–3): Our Consciences Are Free from the Law

§2. We are justified by faith alone. We can come before God with confidence, apart from the law (par. 1). But this does not mean that the law has no role to play in the Christian life: it teaches us even though it no longer condemns us (par. 2).

§3. Calvin expounds this teaching from Galatians.

The Second Part of Christian Freedom (§§4–6): We Obey God Willingly and Freely, Not Constrained by the Law

§4. Justification by law leads to a dread of God's judgment. But justification by faith sets us free from this (as in §§2–3) so that we can now obey God.

§5. God relates to believers not with legal rigor, as a strict judge, but with fatherly gentleness. Calvin applies pastorally the doctrine of double justification. We come to God not as servants from whom full and perfect obedience is required, but as children to a father who is delighted with even the smallest progress of his offspring.

[§6 gives some scriptural evidence for this.]

The Third Part of Christian Freedom (§§7–9): We Are Free in "Things Indifferent"

§7. Our consciences are free from legalistic rules in "indifferent" matters such as those listed on line 1 of p. 839. Once we get caught up in legalistic scruples, we are on a dangerous course (par. 2).

§8. Scriptural support for this freedom. Summary in the last paragraph.

§9. Freedom is not to be taken as a pretext for gluttony or luxury. God gives us his gifts to be used lawfully, with moderation. Most err in this, says Calvin. Above all, we need to learn the secret of being content with our present circumstances.

Freedom and the Weak (§§10–13)

§10. At the bottom of p. 840 Calvin mentions two abuses of Christian freedom: to use it as an excuse for excess (§9) and to use it without regard for the weak (§§10–13). Christian freedom means that we *may* do certain things, not that we *must*. True freedom means partaking or abstaining as circumstances dictate. In particular, it means abstaining rather than causing the weak to stumble.

§11. We must beware giving offense to the weak where we would be guilty of making them stumble (par. 2). This is a scriptural principle (par. 4), *but* we must not give way to Pharisaic legalists who seek to bring others into bondage (par. 3). This is also a scriptural principle (par. 5).

§12. Unless we can distinguish between the weak and legalists, we will lose our Christian freedom. Legalists try to impose rules upon others by posing as the weak. Calvin expounds the difference from Scripture. We must know when to restrain our freedom out of love (par. 1) and when to exercise it (par. 2). The universal principle is love, which seeks our neighbor's edification (par. 3).

§13. We are not to raise tumults in the name of freedom, as did some who exercised it intemperately. But nor are we to tolerate errors like the Roman Catholic Mass on the grounds of not offending the weak.

Freedom and Civil Laws (§§14–16)

§14. Conscience is free from human laws as regards our standing before God.

§15. We need to grasp the (Lutheran) distinction between the two kingdoms/governments/jurisdictions: spiritual versus temporal/political (par. 1). Christian freedom belongs to the spiritual rather than the political order. It does not free us from our duty to obey the law of the land (par. 2). Omit paragraphs 3 to 5.

[§15 (pars. 4 and 5) and §16 each contain a discussion of conscience.]

123

22

Prayer
(3.20.1–14)

Introduction

Calvin's emphasis on usefulness is further illustrated by this lengthy chapter on prayer, longer than the five chapters on the Christian life. He sets out four rules on prayer and expounds the Lord's Prayer.

Questions

Why ought we to pray? In what way ought we to pray?

3.20. Prayer. Footnotes 6, 8, 9, and 17 are of interest.

§1. In Christ, God offers us many blessings (par. 1). But it is of little value to know this if we do not avail ourselves of this through prayer (par. 2).

§2. All to which the gospel points us are treasures we must appropriate by prayer.

§3. But does God need our prayer since he knows everything? Prayer is ordained more for our sake than for his (par. 1). In paragraph 2 Calvin briefly outlines six reasons why we should pray. God often delays his answers to train us to pray (par. 3). The fact of providence does not rule out the need for prayer (par. 4).

Four Rules of Prayer (§§4–16)

§4. The *First Rule* is that when we come to pray, our hearts and minds should be suitably disposed to enter into conversation with God. Calvin urges confidence and intimacy in prayer to God, but leaves no room for the flippancy, casualness, and irreverence so often characteristic of prayer today.

§5. We must resist wandering thoughts in prayer (par. 1). Raising our hands reminds us that we need to raise up our minds to God, setting aside all irrelevant thoughts (par. 2). We should also take care to ask of him no more than he allows. We should seek his will, not our wicked desires (par. 3). All this is beyond our capabilities, so we need the help of the Holy Spirit to pray aright (par. 4).

§6. The *Second Rule* is that when we ask things of God, we should be aware of our insufficiency and filled with an earnest desire to attain what we ask. Thoughtless prayers that do not arise from the heart merely mock God.

§7. We do not always feel our need to the same extent, but there is no time when we have no need to pray. We must always pray for forgiveness of sins and deliverance from temptation. Prayer without repentance is of no value.

§8. The *Third Rule* is that when we pray to God, we should humbly give glory to God alone, giving up all thought of our own glory or worth and without any self-assurance. We pray to God on the basis of his mercy alone, not trusting in our own righteousness.

§9. Prayer must begin with humble confession of guilt and a plea for forgiveness. This is the only basis upon which even the most holy Christian can come before God.

§10. But what of David and others who appealed to their own innocence and righteousness when they prayed? Calvin's doctrine of double justification comes into play here. God does not esteem our prayer according to the merit of our good works, yet those who are conscious of being upright and innocent may derive confirming assurance from that. This should be true for *all believers*.

§11. The *Fourth Rule* is that although we should in humility be aware of our unworthiness, we should nonetheless pray with confidence that God will answer our prayer. This does not mean that we cannot pray if we suffer from doubts or fears. Here, as in his understanding of faith (3.2), Calvin blends a high view of Christian confidence with a realistic grasp of Christian frailties (par. 2). Prayer must be *believing* prayer (par. 3).

§12. It is only because we are aware of God's favor and benevolence toward us that we have the confidence to call upon him. This is known by all who have experienced true prayer (par. 1). It is also in accord with Scripture. Without faith and hope, prayer is vain (par. 2). This does not preclude a deep sense of our own sinfulness (par. 3).

§13. Prayer is both commanded by God's precept and encouraged by his promises. Prayerlessness is therefore both disobedience and unbelief.

§14. Despite God's promises, we are reluctant to pray (par. 1). Prayer is not dependent upon our merit. We may not attain to the holiness of the biblical heroes, but we share a common faith with them. We should approach God with confidence and humility.

[God also answers imperfect prayers. The four rules do not mean that God answers only perfect prayers (§§15–16). We pray in the name of Jesus, our sole Mediator (§§17–20), and do not seek the intercession of the saints (§§21–27). Prayer should be both private and public (§§28–30). Singing is good in worship, so long as we take care "that our ears be not more attentive to the melody than our minds to the spiritual meaning of the words" (§§31–32). Calvin expounds the Lord's Prayer (§§34–49). (Notice the definition of God's kingdom/reign in §42.) Finally, there is value in regular times of prayer (§50), and we should persevere in prayer (§51) while recognizing that the answer may not take the form that we had hoped (§52).]

23

Election and Reprobation (3.21.1–3, 7; 3.22.1–3, 7, 11; 3.23.1–3, 5, 7–8)

Introduction

Why do some believe and others do not? The answer lies not in us but in God's eternal election (chap. 21). The prime basis for this doctrine is the teaching of Scripture (chap. 22). God wills not just the salvation of the elect but also the damnation of the reprobate (chap. 23).

Question

Why does Calvin hold that God ordains who will be saved and who will be lost?

3.21. **Election: Predestination to Salvation/Destruction.** Footnotes 1, 2, 4, and 6 are of interest.

§§1–3. Not all believe or even have the opportunity to believe. Why not? Because of election. This is a *useful* doctrine, says Calvin, for the reasons given at the end of paragraph 1. To deny it is to detract from God's glory and to tear up humility by the roots (par. 2). The doctrine has many benefits (par. 3). There are two dangers to be avoided. The first is curiosity, seeking to know more than God has revealed to us. Calvin is emphatic about the perils of this (ends of §1 and §2). The second is neglect of what God *has* revealed. To suppress the doctrine is to insult the Holy Spirit, who has put it in Scripture because it is necessary and useful (§3).

[§4. Again, "we should not investigate what the Lord has left hidden in secret," nor "neglect what he has brought into the open." §5. God chose the nation of Israel. (At footnote 16 Calvin defines "predestination": "God's eternal decree, by which he compacted with himself what he willed to become of each man.") §6. God also elected individuals within the Israelite nation to eternal salvation.]

§7. God elects individuals to eternal salvation. The first two paragraphs may be skimmed. The last paragraph is an important summary.

3.22. Scriptural Proof for Election. Footnotes 4 and 13 are of interest.

§1. Election is *not* on the basis of foreseen merit. In paragraph 3 Calvin cites Christ as the supreme instance of election, following Augustine. (But this would seem to be a dangerous argument, hinting at adoptionism.) Scripture shows that election is based upon nothing in us (pars. 4 and 5).

§§2–3. Further scriptural proof that election is not based on any foreseen good in us.

[§§4–6 consider the case of Jacob and Esau, from Romans 9–11.]

§7. Christ's own teaching on election, drawn from John.

[Augustine is cited for support (§8). Calvin makes a very confident claim at the end of the first paragraph. Augustine does support Calvin's doctrine of election, but not his doctrine of reprobation (below). In §9 Thomas Aquinas is misrepresented and then chastised. In fact, Thomas came much closer to Calvin than he realized. In §10 Calvin ties together God's universal call in the preaching of the gospel and the particular "effectual calling" of the elect, who are given the gift of faith.]

§11. The theme of reprobation is introduced. Read the closing sentences.

3.23. Reprobation and Objections to It. Footnotes 1, 6, 17, and 18 are of interest.

§1. Election logically implies its converse: reprobation. For Calvin, this means not merely that God passes over/fails to choose the nonelect (Augustine's view), but that he positively wills and ordains their sin and condemnation. Calvin did not invent this idea but was following a strand of late-medieval Augustinian thought, as did Luther and Zwingli.

First Objection: Election Makes God a Tyrant (§§2–5)

§2. An important section. Calvin refers all to God's will as the ultimate cause. "Whatever he wills, by the very fact that he wills it, must be considered righteous." Here he follows late-medieval theology. Duns Scotus and the nominalists argued that no reason could be given for God's will. But the last paragraph gives qualifications. Calvin does not wish to portray an amoral God.

§3. The wicked cannot blame predestination for their damnation since their own manifest sin and guilt have merited it. (But, how did they *become* sinful?)

[In §4 Calvin again refers all to God's will, on the grounds that we are too feeble to penetrate what lies behind it.]

§5. We are not to question God's will. We should believe without understanding.

Second Objection: Election Removes Human Guilt and Responsibility (§§6–9)

[§6. Predestination does not mean that the wicked are not responsible.]

§§7–8. Important sections. God predestined the fall of Adam, for a reason that is beyond our understanding. Calvin's doctrine of providence forces him to say that God did not merely permit the fall, but positively ordained it—his "dreadful decree." Observe the repeated appeal to the doctrine of providence in these sections. But while Adam's fall was ordained by providence, he fell of his own fault (§8, par. 2; also 1.15.8).

[§9. Reaffirmation of human responsibility. Especially see the last sentence.]

[Third Objection: Election Makes God Partial. God's justice is impartial, but his mercy is given according to the good pleasure of his will (§§10–11).]

[Fourth Objection: Election Destroys Zeal for Holiness. Its very goal is holiness of life (§12).]

[Fifth Objection: Election Makes Admonitions Meaningless. Augustine answered this in his book Rebuke and Grace (§§13–14).]

24

Predestination
and the Final Resurrection
(3.24.4–8, 15–17;
3.25.1–3, 6, 10, 12)

Introduction

Calvin examines further how God works in both the elect and
the reprobate (chap. 24). The Christian hope is for bodily resurrection (chap. 25).

Questions

How does election relate to assurance (3.24)? What is the Christian hope for the future (3.25)?

3.24. Election and Reprobation. Footnotes 7, 30, and 33 are of interest.

[§§1–3. God gives us faith, not just the potential to believe (which became the Arminian position).]

§§4–6. Very important sections. In seeking assurance, we should begin with Christ/God's promises, not with predestination.

§4. *Logically* predestination comes first, but in seeking assurance, we do not start by asking whether we are elect. To pry into God's secret will is fatal, because God has never published a list of the elect. But once we know ourselves to be Christians, the knowledge that God has chosen us is a great comfort.

§5. But to find assurance, we *start* with Christ. If we know him, we can be sure that we are elect.

§6. If we are still unsure of this, all we need to do is *now* to embrace him as our Savior (par. 1). Assurance of salvation concerns not just our present state but also our final salvation (par. 2).

§7. But there are many who do not persevere and therefore are lost. These had only a temporary faith, not true saving faith. Observing such people should lead us to avoid arrogant and presumptuous self-confidence. But it should not lessen our "quiet reliance upon the Lord's promise" of final salvation.

§8. There is a general call to all in the preaching of the Word and a special inward call by the Holy Spirit. This latter is given to the elect *and* in a lesser way to temporary believers.

[§9 considers the case of Judas. §§10–11 attack Bucer's idea that there is in the elect from birth a "seed of election." §§12–14 consider God's treatment of the reprobate.]

§§15–16. Calvin considers passages of Scripture that refer to God's desire for all to be saved. He does not take these texts seriously enough, though he allows them a little more weight in his commentaries (e.g., on 2 Pet. 3:9). Calvin concedes that God has a universal will for the salvation of all, as well as his purpose for the salvation of the elect. But his dislike of paradox leads him to resolve this issue by effectively dissolving God's universal will.

§17. Further objections. Predestination does not alter the fact that salvation is received by faith in God's promise. God's will appears to *us* to be double, but in reality it is single. Read the final sentence. Do you agree?

3.25. The Final Resurrection. Footnotes 5, 12, 13, and 26 are of interest.

§§1–2. This is a hard life, so we need future hope to sustain us. We are to focus our minds on the hope of the resurrection. In this chapter Calvin is less Platonist than in 3.9 (e.g.) and sees salvation as bodily resurrection upon Christ's return rather than release from the body at death. The second paragraph of §2 is less important and can be omitted.

§3. We hope for a bodily resurrection. This is hard to believe, but two things can help us. The *first* is the resurrection of Christ. The last three paragraphs are a somewhat dated defense of the historicity of the resurrection and can be omitted.

[**§4.** The *second* help to faith is to consider God's omnipotence. In §5 Calvin attacks various errors and grossly misrepresents those who believed in a millennium.]

§6. The body dies, but the soul survives death and is immortal. Scripture compares the body to a hut from which we depart when we die. In the last paragraph Calvin rejects speculation concerning the intermediate state, setting out his own position in the next-to-last sentence.

[In §§7–8 Calvin insists that it is the *same* body/flesh that rises. God does not merely provide us with a new body. He recognizes, of course, that our resurrection bodies will be transformed. §9 considers the resurrection of the ungodly.]

§10. Eternal life is described in scriptural terms, with the usual rejection of curiosity and speculation. We will not all be equal in heaven.

[**§11.** We should devote our energies to ensuring that we attain to heaven rather than speculating about its exact nature.]

§12. A restrained statement on the nature of hell.

BOOK 4

The External Means or Aids

By Which God Invites Us into the Society
of Christ and Holds Us Therein

Book 3 is devoted to the individual's appropriation of the work of Christ, book 4 to its corporate dimension. The opening chapters (1–2) define the true church and contrast it with the state of the Roman Church. After a chapter (3) expounding the scriptural pattern for Christian ministry, Calvin devotes considerable space to a historical survey of the development of the ministry, focusing on the rise of the papacy (chaps. 4–7). (Book 4 is the longest of the four books, and this is due to the substantial historical material in these chapters.) A key chapter (8) explains how the authority of the church is grounded on and subject to the authority of Scripture. This is followed by a discussion of the authority of church councils (chap. 9) and the role of the church in making laws and exercising discipline (chaps. 10–12). After discussing vows (chap. 13), Calvin turns to the sacraments, expounding his doctrine of the sacraments in general before considering baptism, infant baptism, and the Lord's Supper in particular (chaps. 14–17). As well as expounding his own view, Calvin rejects the Roman Catholic doctrine of the sacrifice of the Mass and also the other five Roman Catholic sacraments (chaps. 18–19). The final chapter (20) sets out Calvin's theory of civil government.

25

The True Church
(4.1.1, 4–17, 21–22)

Introduction

This chapter shows the importance of the church, gives the marks of the church, and argues that one may not leave a church that bears these marks.

Questions

What are the marks of the true church? What is the distinction between the visible and the invisible church? May we ever leave a church to form another church?

4.1. The True Church. Footnotes 1–3, 10, 11, 14, 18, 19, 21, 22, 24, and 27 are of interest.

 §1. Faith is internal, but it needs external aids: the church, the ministry, and the sacraments. God is our Father, but he has entrusted us to the church as our mother. Calvin here echoes Cyprian without actually naming him (see nn. 3, 10).

[In §2 Calvin considers the clause in the Apostles' Creed relating to the church. The church is catholic/universal, and there can never be two or three churches. §3. The creed also refers to the communion of the saints. The church will never fall.]

§4. More on the church as our mother. Outside of the church there is no life, and it is always disastrous to leave the church.

§5. The importance of the ministry. It is God's appointed way of teaching us through human means. This is both a test of our obedience and a concession to our weakness. It is a serious error to despise the ministry (par. 4). It is even more serious to split churches (par. 5). The last two paragraphs may be omitted.

§6. We must neither exaggerate nor minimize the dignity of the ministry.

§7. The distinction between the "invisible church" (the elect of all times) and the "visible church" (the company of professing Christians on earth now). The latter is always mixed, containing elect and hypocrites. Notice the last paragraph.

§8. The church is "invisible" in that we do not know its boundaries: we cannot tell who is elect. This does not matter since God calls us to accept one another not with assurance of faith (i.e., infallible certainty that they are elect) but with judgment of charity (giving one another the benefit of the doubt).

§9. The marks of the church are "the Word of God purely preached *and heard*, and the sacraments administered according to Christ's institution." But *how* purely does the Word need to be preached, and who decides? For the first question, see §12.

Recognize what Calvin does not say. The Anabaptists and some of Calvin's followers included discipline among

the marks. Calvin strongly believed in church discipline
(4.11–12) and put it into practice in Geneva, but he delib-
erately excluded it from the marks of the true church. This
was because that would open the door for folks to break
away from the church on the grounds that the discipline
was too slack for their taste (§§13–20). There is also no
mention of fellowship, a concept that did not figure much
in the sixteenth-century view of the church.

§10. Where these two marks appear, there is a true church,
and in due course there will be fruit. It is a grievous sin to
flout or to leave such a church.

§11. The same points.

§12. We may not leave a church with the marks of a true church
even if it has many faults. This includes nonessential questions of doctrine. Calvin is delightfully vague here. His "essential" doctrines are very essential, and his "nonessential"
doctrines are very peripheral. This leaves it to us to apply
the principle, which is a helpful one. If it had been heeded
more, there would have been fewer splits in the church.

§13. There is even less excuse for leaving the church because
of the impurity of some members' lives. There is and can
be no such thing as a pure church in this life.

§§14–15. This point is defended on the basis of Paul's deal-
ings with Corinth.

§16. To leave the church because of other members is evidence
of pride and arrogance. *God* is their judge. See the last
paragraph.

§17. The church's holiness is as yet incomplete (par. 1). There
is no time since creation when God has not had a church
on earth (par. 2).

[In §§18–20 Calvin argues that the prophets, Christ, and the
apostles did not leave the existing church because of sinners in it. There is no perfect church in this life.]

§21. We need the forgiveness of sins every day, not just once
in baptism.

§22. Ministers have the power of the keys, to be exercised by preaching and through the sacraments, publicly and privately. This was discussed fully in 3.4.9–15.

[§§23–29 oppose the idea that postbaptismal sin cannot be forgiven.]

26

The Roman Church and the Christian Ministry (4.2.1–2, 9–12; 4.3.1–9)

Introduction

The Roman Catholic Church retains some marks of the church, but not its lawful form (chap. 2). The ministry is necessary for the church, and there are four permanent offices of ministry (chap. 3). There follow a number of chapters on the development of the ministry from its early pattern to its state under the papacy: its primitive form (chap. 4), abuses that emerged under the papacy (chap. 5), the false basis of papal claims (chap. 6), and the development of the papacy (chap. 7).

Questions

How does Calvin view the Roman Catholic Church (4.2)? What are the offices of the ministry in the postapostolic church and their functions (4.3)?

4.2. Comparison of the False and the True Church. Footnotes 3, 5, 15, and 16 are of interest.

§1. What can and cannot be tolerated in the church. There can be no compromise over basic apostolic teaching nor over the right use of the sacraments.

§2. The Roman Catholic Church has deformed the ministry, the Lord's Supper, worship, and doctrine. To leave such a body is not to leave the church of Christ. Paragraphs 2–4 are less important.

[**§§3–8.** The Roman Catholic Church is compared to apostate Judaism. It is not schism to leave a "church" that is devoid of Christ's Word, in order to draw near to Christ himself.]

§9. The Roman Catholic Church is like Israel under Jeroboam, except that the idolatry is worse.

§10. If their churches are true churches, Christ's promises are false.

§11. But under the papacy, Christian baptism remained, together with other vestiges of the church. Read the last sentence.

§12. There are churches among the papists—and need to be for the pope to be the Antichrist. There is a remnant of God's people in their churches, and some marks of the church remain, but not the lawful form of the church. Calvin and the other Reformers needed to strike a careful balance on this question. They needed to portray the Roman Church as bad enough to justify separating from it without being guilty of schism, but not so bad that God had left himself totally without witness for several centuries.

4.3. The Doctors and Ministers of the Church. Footnotes 4, 8, and 11 are of interest.

§1. God speaks to us through human mouths. Why? Calvin gives various reasons why this is a good thing: it shows his regard for us, it teaches us humility, and it fosters mutual love and unity.

§2. The ministry is necessary for the church. It is the sinew that holds the church together. Read the last sentence especially.

§3. Scripture commends the dignity of the ministry. Paul and Cornelius both had to wait for a human being to bring them the gospel.

§4. The five offices of Ephesians 4:11. Apostles, prophets, and evangelists were for the early church *and are occasionally revived.* The apostles were pioneer missionaries. (In 4.8.8–9 Calvin considers their unique and unrepeatable role as the original witnesses to Christ.) Prophets no longer exist *or are rare.* Evangelists are second-class apostles. These three offices were for the founding of the church and are raised up again for exceptional situations, as with the Reformation. Pastors and teachers are permanent.

§5. The role of the apostle/evangelist has passed to the pastor; the role of the prophet has passed to the teacher, who has "exactly the same purpose."

§6. Pastors are to preach and to administer the sacraments. Their teaching is to be both public and private. The latter probably embraces what today we would call "pastoral counseling." Later in the section Calvin adds a third element: discipline.

§7. In general pastors are to stay put and not to interfere in one another's churches.

§8. In the New Testament, "bishop" = "presbyter" = "pastor" = "minister." Romans 12 and 1 Corinthians 12 list temporary offices and two permanent ones: government and caring for the poor. (Calvin does not appear to distinguish between spiritual gifts and offices.) The governors are the elders, who share with pastors the responsibility for discipline. (This is discussed further in 4.11.6. There, as in 4.4.1 and 4.11.1, he distinguishes two classes of presbyters: pastors who teach and elders who do not—based on 1 Timothy 5:17.)

§9. The care of the poor is entrusted to the deacons. There are two kinds of deacon.

Note: In 4.3, Calvin mentions *four* permanent offices of ministry: pastors, teachers, elders, and deacons. In the 1536 *Institutes* he had mentioned only *two*: pastors and deacons. In 4.4.1 (1543, left unchanged) he says that Scripture knows *three* orders, by treating pastors and teachers as one order. Clearly Calvin's thought was fluid. Basically he thought in terms of *functions* rather than just offices, which is why he could be less rigid. In his 1541 *Ecclesiastical Ordinances* there are four orders.[1]

[§§10–16 concern the appointment of ministers: the need for proper calling, for the right sort of man; how to appoint, choose, and install ministers.]

[**4.4.** Church Government in the Early Church before the Rise of the Papacy. A history of the development of the ministry: the rise of episcopacy (§§1–4); changes in the diaconate (§§5–9); the selection and ordination of ministers, stressing the need for the consent of the people (§§10–15).]

[**4.5.** How the Ancient Form of Church Government Was Completely Overthrown by the Papal Tyranny. A historical account of the abuses that have emerged in the Roman Catholic Church, such as the appointment of bishops who are unsuitable because of their age or morals (§1), appointment by rulers and without the consent of the people (§§2–3), simony and pluralism (§§6–7), and absenteeism (§§11–12).]

[**4.6.** Roman Primacy. A historical and theological refutation of papal claims. Peter was no pope (§§3–7). The church's sole head is Christ (§§8–10). Peter's primacy would not pass to Rome (§§11–13), and Peter was not the leader of

1. J. K. S. Reid, ed., *Calvin: Theological Treatises*, Library of Christian Classics 22 (London: SCM; Philadelphia: Westminster, 1954), 58–66.

the Roman church (§§14–15). Rome enjoyed a primacy of honor but no papal powers (§§16–17).]

[4.7. The Origin and Growth of the Papacy. A historical account of the rise of the papacy from the fourth century and its perversion of the church. The pope is the Antichrist prophesied in Scripture (§§24–25).]

27

The Authority of the Church
(4.8)

Introduction

The church has authority to define doctrine, but only in line with the teaching of the Bible, which is the written Word of God (chap. 8). What is true of the church in general is true of councils in particular (chap. 9).

Question

What sort of authority does the church have?

4.8. **The Power of the Church in Matters of Doctrine.** Footnote 13 is of interest.

   §1. The doctrinal authority of the church lies in laying down articles of faith and in explaining them (par. 1). Christ alone is the schoolmaster of the church (par. 2). The power of the church is "to be not grudgingly manifested but yet to be kept within definite limits"; otherwise tyranny soon follows (par. 3).

§2. Authority belongs not to people personally but to their ministry, meaning to the Word of God, whose ministry is entrusted to the leaders.

§3. The Old Testament prophets spoke only the words that God had given them. "They had holy and pure lips when they began to be instruments of the Holy Spirit."

§4. Similarly, the apostles "are not to prate whatever they please, but are faithfully to report the commands of him by whom they have been sent." The church's power is "not infinite but subject to the Lord's Word" and limited by it.

§5. In Old Testament times, God never manifested himself in any other way than through the Son. But he did this in a variety of ways during this time.

§6. On the writing of the Old Testament Scriptures.

§7. God's supreme and final revelation is in Jesus Christ (Heb. 1:1–2).

§8. Only the Bible is to be accepted in the church as the Word of God. The only authorized standard for church teaching is that Word. The apostles wrote the New Testament "with Christ's Spirit as precursor in a certain measure dictating the words." Calvin often referred to the Holy Spirit as "dictating" the Scriptures, but he also made it clear that he believed in their genuine human authorship. The human authors wrote freely, and each book reflects the style of its author, but what ensues is exactly what God intended—contrary to footnote 7.

§9. An important section. The sovereign power of pastors is "that they may dare boldly to do all things by God's Word." They have real authority but not independent of God's Word (par. 1). The difference between the apostles and all who follow them is that while the apostles were "sure and genuine scribes of the Holy Spirit" so that their writings are to be seen as oracles of God, the task of their successors is merely to teach what is found in Scripture (par. 2). (For

149

footnote 9, see comment on footnote 7, above.) The church does not have liberty to coin new doctrines but must stick with the teaching of Scripture (par. 2). This applies to the universal church as well as to individuals (par. 3).

§10. Attack on the Roman Catholic view that makes councils infallible and allows the church to coin new doctrines.

§11. The Roman Catholic Church claims to be led by the Spirit. The Spirit does lead the church, but we must test all such claims by the Word (see 1.9).

§12. Answer to Roman Catholic appeals to Ephesians 5:26–27 and 1 Timothy 3:15.

§13. Important. The Roman Catholic view implies that the Spirit leads the church *without the Word*. Calvin insists that Word and Spirit be held together (as in 1.9). The leading of the Spirit and the authority of the church must never be divorced from the Word of God. All that we should expect from the Spirit of Christ is that he will enlighten our minds to grasp the truth of Christ's teaching.

§14. Tradition may not add to the teaching of Scripture, which is complete and perfect.

§15. The church has authority to teach God's Word.

§16. Refutation of Roman Catholic examples of tradition adding to Scripture.

[4.9. The Authority of Councils. Like the church in general, councils have authority, but only when they follow God's Word. Calvin explicitly approves the doctrinal decisions of the first four ecumenical councils (§8, par. 2): Nicaea (AD 325), Constantinople (381), Ephesus (431), and Chalcedon (451). But all decisions of councils need to be tested by Scripture.]

28

Church Discipline
(4.11.1–3, 5; 4.12.1–11)

Introduction

The church has the power to make laws, but not apart from God's Word and not so as to undermine Christian freedom (chap. 10). The church also has the power to discipline morals, based on the sanction of excommunication (chap. 11). Calvin gives detailed instructions as to how discipline should and should not be exercised (chap. 12). Caution should be exercised in making vows, especially vows of celibacy (chap. 13).

Questions

What is the power of the keys entrusted to the church? Why and how should discipline be exercised in the church?

[4.10. The Church's Power to Make Laws. Calvin opposes the Roman Catholic Church for imposing laws that destroy

Christian freedom. "Necessity ought not to be imposed upon consciences in those matters from which they have been freed by Christ" (§1, par. 3). The church has no right to enforce laws apart from God's Word. "Some form of organization is necessary in all human society to foster the common peace and maintain concord" (§27, par. 2), but such laws should be few and not treated as necessary for salvation. Ceremonies should be few and simple and point us straight to Christ.]

4.11. The Jurisdiction of the Church. Footnotes 2, 3, 6, and 9 are of interest.

§1. Jurisdiction is the third part of ecclesiastical power (see 4.8.1): the church's power lies in doctrine (4.8–9), legislation (4.10), and jurisdiction (4.11–12). Jurisdiction pertains to the discipline of morals. This requires courts of judgment. There are two types of presbyter (see the notes on 4.3.8, above). The church's power in this area rests upon the keys entrusted to it in Matthew 18:15–18. This is not to be confused with the *doctrinal* authority entrusted to the church in Matthew 16:19 and John 20:23, which refers to the ministry of the Word.

§2. Matthew 18:15–18: the power of binding and loosing refers to the discipline of excommunication. The judgment of the church here is the proclamation of God's sentence.

§3. Church discipline was not temporary, until such time as Christian rulers should arise. There is a fundamental difference between civil and ecclesiastical power, and they should not be confused.

[**§4.** The discipline instituted by Christ in Matthew 18 was not intended to be temporary.]

§5. Paragraph 2 gives the twofold aim of jurisdiction and names two things to take into account. The first is considered in paragraph 3, the second in §6. Excommunication is the church's ultimate sanction, the "final thunderbolt."

[§§6–16. Attack on Roman Catholic abuses of excommunication and on the Roman Catholic Church's usurpation of temporal/secular power.]

4.12. Church Discipline. Footnotes 1, 2, 4, 5, and 8 are of interest.

§1. Discipline is based on the power of the keys and upon spiritual jurisdiction, as set out in 4.11. Paragraph 2 stresses the vital need for discipline. Where does that leave our churches today? But observe also the importance of mildness and gentleness.

§2. Four stages of church discipline.

§3. With open, public sins, one should proceed at once to public response.

§4. Serious sins call for more than admonition or rebuke.

§5. The three aims of discipline, one per paragraph.

§6. Public and private sins call for different treatment.

§7. The practice of the early church.

§8. The need for moderation and gentleness, in line with the aims of discipline. The early fathers erred here (par. 2). Paragraph 3 may be omitted.

§9. We must not write off those under discipline. We should regard them as only temporarily cut off from the church.

§10. Excommunication merely warns of damnation *if* they do not repent.

§11. Discipline is important but is not a ground for dividing the church.

[§12 opposes the Anabaptists, who like the Donatists split the church over discipline. Discernment is needed in discipline (§13). §§14–21 deal with the use and abuse of fasting, which is defined in §18. The clergy need a stricter discipline (§22), but imposing clerical celibacy is quite wrong and leads to all sorts of abuses (§§23–28). Recent experience in a number of countries, especially Ireland and the United States, confirms the truth of the last statement.]

153

[4.13. Vows. We should be very careful before making rash vows, although there is a place for sober and temporary vows. "Celibacy holds the first place for insane boldness" (§3, par. 2) since "celibacy is one thing, virginity another" (§3, par. 3). Especially rash are monastic vows (§§8–21). Calvin is biting in his attack on contemporary monastic abuses. He also confesses that he is unhappy even with the purest form of monasticism (§16).]

29

The Sacraments in General
(4.14.1, 3–9, 12, 14–17, 19–20, 23)

Introduction

A sacrament is a "visible word" in which the same grace is offered as through the gospel and is received by faith (chap. 14). Baptism and the Lord's Supper are the only ordinary sacraments, though ordination can also be called a sacrament (chap. 19).

Questions

What is a sacrament? What does God do through the sacraments?

4.14. The Sacraments. Footnotes 1, 2, 13, 15, 18, and 41 are of interest.

> **§1.** The sacraments are aids to faith. Various definitions are given in paragraph 2.
>
> [§2. The origins of the word "sacrament" in the early church.]

155

§3. A sacrament is a sign appended to God's promise. This he does for our benefit, because we are bodily creatures who need to be taught by more than just words.

§4. Sacrament = Word and sign. But the "Word" is not just a mumbled prayer. The "Word" is the preaching of the promise that is attested by the sign.

§5. Calvin opposes the objection that the sign is unnecessary if we already have the Word. Sacraments "represent [God's promises] for us as painted in a picture from life."

§6. The sacrament is a sign of God's covenant, a "visible word," God's promises "portrayed graphically," a mirror in which we see God's grace.

§7. Through the sacraments, as through the Word, God's grace is *offered* to all, but *received* only by faith. The sacraments serve to strengthen our faith. We all need them because our faith is always imperfect, as in Mark 9:24.

§8. More on our need to grow in faith. This is also the work of the Holy Spirit. The last three sentences relate together Word, sacrament, and Holy Spirit.

§9. The sacraments are made effective only when the Holy Spirit works through them.

[In §§10–11 Calvin continues to teach that it is the Holy Spirit who makes both Word and sacrament effective by awakening faith in us.]

§12. God uses sacraments to feed us spiritually, just as he feeds us bodily through food.

[In §13 Calvin debates with Zwingli concerning the meaning of the Latin term *sacramentum*.]

§14. Roman Catholic teaching on the automatic efficacy of the sacraments is wrong. Sacraments bestow no benefit where there is no faith. Read the last paragraph.

§15. Augustine rightly distinguishes between the sacrament itself and the matter of the sacrament (that which it signifies). An example of this is baptism versus regeneration.

156

The unworthy recipient receives the sacrament (sign), but not the matter (what is signified).

§16. *Christ* is the "matter" of the sacraments. Christ is held out to us and offered to us through the sacraments. He is *offered* to all but *received* only by believers. At the end Calvin names two "vices" to be avoided: the Zwinglian and the Roman Catholic errors, respectively.

§17. The sacraments have the same office/function as the Word: to offer Christ to us. This offer is accepted/rejected by faith/unbelief. In the next-to-last paragraph, Calvin represents his view as the "mean" between the errors of Rome and Zwingli.

[§18. There is a wider use of the word "sacrament" to include things like the tree of life, Noah's rainbow, and Gideon's fleece.]

§19. The present discussion is about the sacraments that are intended for ongoing use in the church. We need the regular use of sacraments, of ceremonies that function as signs.

§20. A summary of the sacraments of Old and New Testaments. Calvin here does not exclude calling ordination a sacrament. Old and New Testament sacraments point to the same promises of God in Christ. The sole difference between them is stated in the last sentence.

[In §21 Calvin expounds the Old Testament sacraments further. In §22 he argues that the New Testament sacraments present Christ more clearly than did the Old Testament sacraments.]

§23. Calvin rejects the Roman Catholic view of the difference between Old and New Testament sacraments, as stated in the first sentence. He argues that both Old and New Testament sacraments have the same efficacy.

[The same point is further argued in §§24–26.]

[4.19. The Five Falsely Termed Sacraments. There are only two sacraments, defined as a God-appointed seal to a promise (§§1–3). Roman Catholic confirmation is no true sacra-

157

ment, though there is a need for the early church practice of catechesis leading to confession of faith and laying on of hands (§§4–13). Penance is not a sacrament, though the early church practice was generally good (§§14–17). Extreme unction is not a sacrament (§§18–21). The Roman Catholic practice of ordination is a mockery of the real thing (§§22–33). But properly practiced, ordination *may* be called a sacrament (§§28, 31; see 4.14.20). Marriage is a God-given ordinance, but not a sacrament (§§34–37).]

30

Baptism and Infant Baptism
(4.15.1–6, 13–15;
4.16.1–9, 17, 19–22)

Introduction

Baptism points us to Christ and the benefits that he brings, which are received by faith (chap. 15). Just as infants were circumcised, so may they be baptized since they are not excluded from salvation (chap. 16). Calvin's exposition starts with believers' baptism, which is taken as the norm, and then proceeds to infant baptism. This is in contrast to most of his contemporaries, who simply assumed that infant baptism was the norm.

Questions

What is baptism (4.15)? What does it do? Why should infants receive it (4.16)?

4.15. Baptism. Footnotes 3, 5, 9, and 24 are of interest.

§1. The definition is in the first sentence. Calvin goes on to outline its benefits. In paragraph 2 he denies that baptism is merely a chance for us to confess our faith.

§2. Baptism seals to us the message/promise of the Word. It thus points us to Christ.

§3. We are baptized for *all* our sins, not just *past* sins. But this does not mean (par. 2) that believers can therefore sin with impunity.

§§4–6. Baptism points us to the cleansing of our sins in Christ's blood (§4); to mortification, regeneration, and new life (§5); and, above all, to Christ, through whom alone we enjoy these benefits (§6).

[John the Baptist gave Christian baptism (§§7–8). Baptism is foreshadowed in the Old Testament (§9). It does not remove original sin (§10). We need to fight sin all our lives (§§11–12).]

§13. Baptism is an opportunity for us to confess our faith (though it must not be viewed *merely* as our confession of faith [§1, par. 2]).

§14. We are to receive baptism as from the hand of God. We should look beyond the sign to the realities which it symbolizes.

§15. In Acts, baptism was a confirmation or strengthening of faith. As with all the sacraments, we receive its benefits only by faith.

[Baptism is not invalidated by the unworthiness of the baptizer (§16) or by the fact that faith and repentance may not come until years later (§17). Acts 19:1–7 refers to baptism of the Holy Spirit and does not justify rebaptism with water (§18). Originally baptism was by immersion, but the mode of baptism is unimportant (§19, par. 3). Only ministers are to baptize—and certainly not women (§§20–22)!]

4.16. Infant Baptism. Footnotes 1, 5, 10, 14–16, and 30 are of interest.

§1. Infant baptism needs a defense. (As true today as in Calvin's time.)

§2. If we are to judge this issue rightly, we must pay attention not just to the sign but to the realities to which it points. (Summary of 4.15.4–6, 13.)

§§3–6. Argument from circumcision.

§3. Circumcision is the seal upon God's promises of forgiveness of sins and so forth, just as is baptism.

§4. Thus the promise is the same in both; it is only the outward ceremony that differs. So baptism has replaced circumcision.

§5. If children could be circumcised, they can be baptized; if they can be partakers in the benefits portrayed by circumcision, so also with baptism. Nine lines up from the bottom of the first paragraph on p. 1328, "the word 'baptism'" should be "the word [i.e., promise or substance] of baptism."

§6. There is one covenant [of grace], and the only difference in initiation lies in the outward sign.

§7. Jesus welcomed babes and children. Calvin argues that this *is* significant, even though baptism is not mentioned.

§8. Scripture records no instances of infant baptism or of women receiving communion. This question needs to be decided by the *theology* of baptism, not by the mention or otherwise of infants being baptized in New Testament times.

§9. A summary of the benefits to be derived from infant baptism, benefits for the parents and for the children.

[**§§10–16.** Answer to the Anabaptist denial of the parallel between baptism and circumcision. Colossians 2:11–12 means that the substance of circumcision and of baptism is the same since they signify the same thing (§11). Christians are heirs of the Abrahamic promises (§§13–15). So we should hold to the similarity between baptism and circumcision (§16).]

§17. Children *can* be regenerated.

[§18. Christ was sanctified from earliest infancy, which proves that no age is incapable of receiving sanctification.]

§§19–20. Infants cannot hear the Word, repent, or believe, but this does not prevent God from working in them. That which Luther too rashly *affirmed* (that infants believe) is not impossible. Anyway, if infants' inability to repent or believe excludes them from receiving baptism, it should have excluded them from receiving circumcision. Calvin's point is that *some* of the Anabaptist arguments against infant baptism, if valid, would prove that it was wrong to circumcise infants; yet we know that God commanded just that.

§21. Infants grow into an appreciation of their baptism.

§22. Infants are not excluded from salvation and therefore not from baptism.

[§§23–32. Further arguments. The fact that adults were called to believe before being baptized does not prove that infants cannot be baptized (§23). Abraham believed before circumcision; Isaac did not (§24). Baptism is not essential for salvation (§26). Calvin responds to twenty specific objections raised by Servetus (§§30–31). Infant baptism provides an incentive to instruct our children in the faith (§32).]

31

The Lord's Supper
(4.17.1–5, 8–11, 16, 19, 21, 24, 26, 31–33)

Introduction

In the Lord's Supper the body and blood of Christ are offered to all and are received by faith when the Holy Spirit unites us to them. The bread and wine are not empty symbols, but neither do they become or enclose the body and blood of Christ (chap. 17). The Roman doctrine of the Mass as a sacrifice offered to God is a blasphemy against Christ because it undermines the sufficiency of his unique sacrifice on the cross (chap. 18).

Questions

What happens in the Lord's Supper? How does Calvin differentiate his position from those of Luther and Zwingli?

4.17. The Lord's Supper. Footnotes 1–3, 5, 14, 17, 24, 27, 54, 82, plus (for §§32–33) 9, 11, and 12 are of interest.

Statement of Calvin's Position (§§1–5 [par. 1])

§1. By this sacrament, God nourishes us. The bread and the wine are signs of the spiritual food we receive from Christ's flesh and blood. Just as the bread and wine nourish our bodies, so Christ feeds our souls. The Lord's Supper is a renewal or continuation of the new covenant.

§2. The Lord's Supper strengthens our assurance. The recapitulation/second Adam theme appears in the (long) last sentence. See also the top of p. 1364 (§4) and 2.12.2.

§3. The bread and wine proclaim to us Christ's body and blood, given for our salvation and as food for our souls.

§4. The Supper seals to us the promise of John 6:55–56. We there feed upon him.

§5 (par. 1). The Supper offers us the *same* grace as does the gospel: Christ and his benefits (second and last sentences). Though the Supper thus is a special means of grace, it is not a means of special grace: what is given there is also found elsewhere. But the Supper does this *more clearly* (sent. 2). The Supper points to a feeding on Christ which we enjoy "continually" (sent. 3). In the Supper, preaching is reinforced by a visual (and tangible and edible) aid. The benefit of the Supper is one that we enjoy continually, not just when we hear the Word preached or receive the sacrament.

Rejection of Zwingli's Mere Symbolism (§§5 [par. 2]–11)

§5 (par. 2). Calvin refers to "two faults": the Zwinglian and the Lutheran. He then turns to attack Zwingli. For Zwingli, to believe *is* to eat Christ's flesh. For Calvin, we eat Christ's flesh *by* believing. For Calvin, faith leads to a real communion with/participation in Christ's flesh. Notice the last sentence.

[In §6 Calvin appeals to Augustine and Chrysostom. In §28 he modestly claims that Augustine "is wholly and incontrovertibly on our side." Zwingli, Luther, and the Roman Catholics also appealed to Augustine. This was possible partly because Augustine's position is complex and partly because he was not writing to answer sixteenth-century questions. In §7 Calvin rejects the Zwinglian idea that in the Supper we partake of the Spirit only, not of Christ's flesh and blood.]

§8. Christ is our life. He dwells within us, and we feed upon him, as in John 6.

§9. The importance of partaking of Christ's life-giving flesh and blood. Read the last sentence of each paragraph.

§10. Important section. Our souls are fed by Christ's flesh and blood (par. 1). But since Christ's body is in heaven, how can this happen? We do not bodily ascend to heaven, and he does not bodily descend, but the Holy Spirit bridges the gap (par. 2). (For a helpful analogy of this, see the notes on §12, below.) Because of this work of the Spirit, the Supper is not "a vain and empty sign," but through it we feed on Christ (par. 3). The bread and wine are symbols, but not empty or lying symbols: they give to us that which they symbolize (par. 4).

§11. Final attack on Zwingli. In the Supper we enjoy true participation in Christ himself and thereby the benefits outlined in the last sentence of paragraph 2.

In his attack on Zwingli (§§5–11), Calvin portrays the Supper as a mystery beyond our understanding. As he turns to attack Rome and Luther, the emphasis shifts as he rejects their "absurdities."

Rejection of Roman Catholic Doctrine of Transubstantiation (§§12–15)

[In §§12–15 Calvin attacks medieval developments from the eleventh century onward. §14. Transubstantiation is contrary to "not only Scripture but even the consensus of the ancient church" (§14, par. 2). In §12 Calvin gives a very helpful illustration. How can we here on earth enjoy a true communion with Christ's body and blood, which are in heaven? The sun remains millions of miles from the earth, yet through the mediation of the sun's rays, we enjoy a real communion with the sun, without which there would be no life on earth.]

Rejection of Luther's Doctrine of Local Presence (§§16–19)

§16. Calvin attacks the Lutheran idea of Christ's presence "in, with, and under" the bread and wine. This is wrong because it makes Christ's body ubiquitous (omnipresent), contrary to its nature as a human body (cf. §24). The Lutherans are right to maintain that we communicate with Christ's body, but wrong to imagine that this requires his descent into the bread (see §10). Calvin accuses them of making Christ's body *locally* present (final sentences of §16), a charge to which Luther himself was vulnerable but which was denied by the later Lutheran Formula of Concord (1577).

[**§17.** This is contrary to the true humanity of Christ. **§18.** In the Supper we are lifted up to heaven, where Christ is, through the Spirit.]

§19. We must not undermine the true humanity of Christ's body (against Luther). But at the same time we must hold to a "true and substantial partaking" of Christ (against Zwingli). Observe the grounds on which this is defended in paragraph 3: Scripture; nothing absurd/obscure/ambiguous; true piety and sound edification.

Meaning of "This Is My Body" (§§20–25)

[In §20 Calvin meets the charge that *he* twists these words by charging the Lutherans and the Roman Catholics of just that. In the final paragraph he makes it clear that he sees the bread and wine as more than mere symbols.]

§21. The words should be taken as a *metonymy*, which is explained by examples. On page 1386, line 12 should read: "Today bread is called the body of Christ."

[§§22–23 discuss further the meaning of the word "is." It cannot be literal. Lutherans talk of accepting Christ's words with simple faith, but "the only question is whether it is a crime to investigate the true sense of his words" (par. 5).]

§24. Calvin defends himself against the charge that Luther made against Zwingli: measuring doctrine by human reason. In the first and the third paragraphs, he shows how far he is from being a rationalist. In the last paragraph he turns to the attack. The issue is not what God *could* do but what he *willed* to do. Here Calvin plays the trump card of the Reformed: he appeals to Christ's true humanity.

In paragraph 3 and elsewhere in this chapter, Calvin talks of being quickened by "the substance of his flesh and of his blood." What does he mean by this very "realistic" talk about "substance"? Wendel argues that this means simply the *benefits* that proceed from Christ's flesh and blood.[1] This may or may not be true, but the fact remains that, according to Calvin, we enjoy these benefits only through a real *communion* with his flesh and blood, by the Holy Spirit.[2]

[§25. Further defense of Calvin's "moderate" interpretation of Christ's words.]

Rejection of Ubiquity (§§26–30)

§26. The ascension of Christ and his own words show that his body is now in heaven and not on earth in a bodily manner. This conclusion is drawn from Scripture, not from human reason. At Marburg, Luther said that Zwingli's

---

1. Wendel, *Calvin*, 341–42.
2. For a discussion of this issue, see A. N. S. Lane, "Was Calvin a Crypto-Zwinglian?" in *Adaptations of Calvinism in Reformation Europe: Essays in Honour of Brian G. Armstrong*, ed. M. Holt (Aldershot [Hants]: Ashgate, 2007), 21–41.

appeal to Matthew 26:11 was the best argument that he managed to produce.[3]

[Calvin defends his interpretation of the ascension from Scripture (§27) and from Augustine (§28). He again appeals to Christ's true humanity and rejects the idea of the ubiquity of his body (§§29–30).]

Statement of Calvin's Position (§§31–34)

§31. Calvin insists that he believes as strongly as any Lutheran in Christ's presence in the Supper and our union with Christ. The difference lies only in the "manner" in which this happens: they make Christ descend into the bread and wine while Calvin holds that the Holy Spirit unites us with Christ's body and blood in heaven.

§32. Important for Calvin's attitude to reason. In the first paragraph he confesses faith in what he experiences but cannot understand—a passage foreign to Zwingli's spirit. (Note that what Calvin cannot comprehend is the question of *how* communion with Christ's flesh and blood takes place, not the *fact* of our communion with his flesh and blood. It is not the doctrine of the Lord's Supper that is incomprehensible to Calvin but the mechanics of it.) In the second paragraph he rejects Lutheran absurdities because they are contrary not to reason but to sound Christology. In the third and fourth paragraphs he appeals to faith, as opposed to "the reason of this world." The last paragraph says that we are fed "from the substance of his flesh" (cf. the notes on §24, above).

§33. Calvin affirms his belief in our partaking of Christ's flesh and blood through the Spirit. *This* is the important point about the Supper. But the Lutherans overlook this and devote all their attention to their belief in Christ's real presence in, with, and under the elements (par. 1). Calvin

3. Collin's Report on the Marburg Colloquy in M. E. Lehmann, ed., *Luther's Works*, vol. 38 (Philadelphia: Fortress, 1971), 58–59.

speaks of *spiritual* eating because it is through the Spirit. Paragraph 3 meets the charge that Calvin speaks only of enjoying the *benefits* of Christ's body and blood (cf. the notes on §24, above). From paragraph 4 onward, Calvin considers the case of the wicked communicant. Christ's body and blood are *offered* to all but actually *received* only by believers (against the Lutheran view).

[§34 appeals to Augustine and Cyril on this point.]

[§§35–50. Adoration of the elements is idolatry (§§35–37). The Lord's Supper points us to mutual love (§38) and should not be celebrated without preaching (§39). It is to be received worthily, which means with faith and with love; yet this sacrament "is ordained not for the perfect, but for the weak and feeble" (§§40–42). It should be celebrated "very often, and at least once a week" (§43), and believers should receive communion frequently (§§44–46). Denying the cup to the laity (so-called communion in one kind) is wrong (§§47–50).]

[4.18. The Papal Mass a Sacrilege. The Mass is defined as "a work by which the priest who offers up Christ, and the others who participate in the oblation, merit God's favor, or it is an expiatory victim, by which they reconcile God to themselves" (§1, par. 2). This doctrine is a blasphemy against Christ because it undermines the full and perfect sufficiency of the cross and the uniqueness of Christ's priesthood, as taught in Hebrews (§§2–3, 5). After the cross, there is no more room for sacrifices for sins (like the Mass), only for sacrifices of thanksgiving, as often taught in the New Testament. (§13 offers definitions of different types of sacrifice.) The Lord's Supper is a gift that we receive from God, not something we offer to God by way of payment (§7). Baptism and the Lord's Supper are the only two sacraments instituted by God, and the church should rest content with these two (§§19–20).]

[For 4.19, "The Five Falsely Termed Sacraments," see the end of chapter 29, above.]

32

Civil Government
(4.20.1–4, 6, 8–9, 14–16, 22–25, 30–32)

Introduction

Civil government is instituted by God, and rulers are to be obeyed.

Questions

What is the role of rulers? May they ever be disobeyed?

4.20. Civil Government. Footnotes 2, 4, 7, 20–22, 36, 39, 53–54, and 56 are of interest.

§1. There is a twofold government: the civil/political and the spiritual/eternal—Luther's "two kingdoms" (cf. 3.19.15). We must not confuse the spiritual kingdom of Christ with civil government. To seek to confine the former within this-worldly structures is a "Jewish vanity."

§2. The two governments are distinct, but not at variance. Civil government is God-given and has vital functions in this life. In the middle of the section, Calvin makes an important statement about the "appointed end" of civil government. This includes the protection of true religion.

§3. Anabaptist anarchy is lunacy. The last two paragraphs outline the structure of the chapter.

§4. Scriptural proof that the office of rulers is appointed by God. May be skimmed, but notice the last sentence, Calvin's conclusion.

[§5 attacks Anabaptist anarchism.]

§6. Magistrates need to see themselves as God's vicars or deputies and behave accordingly.

[§7 gives further scriptural proof that the office of ruler is ordained by God.]

§8. Different forms of government. Calvin favors a blend of aristocracy and democracy. But *whatever* form of government we live under, we must be compliant and obedient (last sentence).

§9. Rulers are to be concerned for religion as well as for secular affairs, for the first as well as the second table of the law. The fourth paragraph may be omitted.

[§10. Rulers need to punish offenders, and in doing so they carry out *God's* judgment. §§11–12. Just wars are lawful. §13. Rulers may raise taxes.]

§14. The importance of good laws. What of the law of Moses? Should the law of the land follow it, as some are suggesting today? Calvin follows the traditional division of the law of Moses into three: moral, ceremonial, and judicial.

§15. The moral law is eternal and unchanging. The ceremonial law was for the Jews, until the reality came in Christ. The judicial law was for the people of Israel, but it teaches us principles of justice and equity. We are bound by the *principles* underlying the judicial law but not by the laws themselves.

§16. Equity is universal: Calvin equates the moral law with natural law and conscience. But the forms of the law, and especially the punishments, must vary with circumstances.

[§§17–21. Law courts are legitimate in principle, but only when used with love.]

§§22–25. Subjects are to honor, reverence, and obey their rulers, as God's representatives. (The honor is due to the *office* and is not based on the worthiness of the occupant, who may be a contemptible person.) Experience shows that many rulers are wicked and unworthy. Such a ruler is to be seen as God's judgment upon us and is to be obeyed fully.

[§§26–29. Scriptural proof that even the worst rulers are appointed by God and are to be honored and obeyed.]

§30. It is not for us to rise up against unjust rulers. We must trust God, who has his own ways of getting rid of them.

§31. But there *is* a place for subordinate rulers (not private citizens) to remove tyrants.

§32. *Passive* disobedience is allowed where rulers command something contrary to God's law.

Appendix

Table of Reading Lengths

To aid those using this reader in the classroom, the table below tells approximately how many pages of the McNeill-Battles (MB) edition of Calvin's Institutes are covered in each reading. Longer readings (such as reading 7) include suggestions within the chapter about which paragraphs can be omitted to shorten the reading.

Reading number	Reading title	*Institutes* reference	MB pages
1	Introductory Material	pp. 3–8; "Prefatory Address"	17½
2	Knowing God and Ourselves	1.1–4	16
3	God Revealed in Creation	1.5	16
4	The Bible and the Holy Spirit	1.6–9	17½
5	Idolatry and the Trinity	1.11–13	16½
6	The Created World and Humanity as Created	1.14–15	19

Reading number	Reading title	*Institutes* reference	MB pages
7	God's Sovereign Providence	1.16–18	28½
8	Original Sin	2.1–2.3.5	17
9	How God Works in the Human Heart	2.3.6–2.5	18
10	The Place of the Law	2.6–7	18
11	Exposition of the Moral Law	2.8	18
12	Relation between the Old and New Testaments	2.9–11	16
13	The Person of Jesus Christ	2.12–14	11
14	The Redemptive Work of Jesus Christ	2.15–17	25½
15	Saving Faith	3.1–2	17
16	Regeneration and Repentance	3.3–5	16
17	The Christian Life: Self–Denial	3.6–7	16½
18	The Christian Life: Bearing Our Cross and Attitude toward This Life	3.8–10	17½
19	Justification by Faith	3.11.1–3.14.8	16½
20	The Value of Our Good works	3.14.9–3.18	15½
21	The True Nature of Christian Freedom	3.19	13½
22	Prayer	3.20	20
23	Election and Reprobation	3.21–23	20
24	Predestination and the Final Resurrection	3.24–25	22
25	The True Church	4.1	19
26	The Roman Church and the Christian Ministry	4.2–7	15
27	The Authority of the Church	4.8–9	16½
28	Church Discipline	4.10–13	16
29	The Sacraments in General	4.14; 4.19	16
30	Baptism and Infant Baptism	4.15–16	21½
31	The Lord's Supper	4.17–18	21½
32	Civil Government	4.20	21

Made in the USA
Columbia, SC
01 December 2021